ISBN: 0-385-04605-7
Library of Congress Catalog Card Number 72–97091
Copyright © 1973 by Farm Journal, Inc.
Printed in the United States of America

How to Run Your House
without letting it run you

Edited by JEAN GILLIES
Home Management Editor, FARM JOURNAL

Drawings by BONNIE SARGENT

Doubleday & Company, Inc., Garden City, New York

CONTENTS

One Thousand Authors

That's right! One thousand women have written this book. They are homemakers all over the country who have sent their tips for easier homemaking to FARM JOURNAL magazine. They have shared ideas on keeping up with a house, yard, husband, children and unexpected guests—ideas from stretching storage space in closets to making a heart-shaped cake without a special mold. We published their best ideas to help other homemakers. In addition, women editors of FARM JOURNAL have visited almost every state, gathering more little work-easers.

Now, we've selected the best of these home-tested bits of advice and shortcuts and have organized them into a book. Read the first chapter to get a total look at your job of home-making. It will help you put your work into proper perspective, and help you decide on what is most important. Then browse through the rest of the book; keep it handy for reference. We suggest you try one new idea a day to help you run your house—and your life—without letting them run you!

"Don't take dust too seriously. There is no better way to make your family and yourself miserable than to have the house so spotless that everyone is afraid to sit down on a chair or touch a table or walk across the room with his shoes on."

Keep Cool

Keep Cool

Decide what is important to you—
and concentrate on those things

Of course, you can keep cool. It's not always easy, and it takes determination. But there are homemakers around the country who say it can be done—and they tell you how.

Not long ago, a frustrated young mother wrote: "Help! I never can get all my work done. I've reached the breaking point! Tell me, how do other women manage?"

FARM JOURNAL printed her panic letter and hundreds of women—from brides to grandmothers—responded with sympathy, encouragement and solid advice. Their combined wisdom offers help in looking at the total job of homemaking. Whether you are a seasoned homemaker or a brand new bride, they have some ideas for you.

YOUNG MOTHER BLUES

The early years of marriage can be especially trying. It's when your first youngsters are in the help-me stage and your home and equipment are not the latest. To top it off, you may be learning basic homemaking skills. "I think I shed an oceanful of tears in the first year of our married life," one New York State woman recalls. "How many batches of cookies and johnnycakes I threw out, no one will ever know." So, just remember that you are not alone in your frustrations.

And things do get better. "The next 10 years will bring you more conveniences. Your children will be older and can help themselves (and help you, if you guide them). You'll achieve cooking and housekeeping competence that only experience can give you," consoles an Illinois homemaker. Meanwhile, work on improving what you can, and don't expect too much of yourself.

BE REALISTIC

Stop trying to be ideal. "I was known as a perfectionist," a Nebraska woman writes. "On washday, all the socks had to hang on the line identically—in pairs, by the heels, to the right. All cup handles in a cupboard had to point in the same direction so they could be grabbed quickly. Gradually, I learned to relax. Certainly I wouldn't be remembered for my cup handles—or would I? This letting-go takes self-discipline, but relaxed standards mean a more relaxed you."

Stop competing with relatives and neighbors, too. "I used to admire one gal's weedless garden, another's spotless home, a third's freezerful of everything yummy. I added reading, sewing and decorating that I'd like to do, until the total was enough to panic an old pro," says a South Dakota homemaker. Find your talent —maybe making apple pie or cinnamon rolls —and specialize in it.

Expect your house to be somewhat messy as long as little children live in it. "Tell your-

"Here's a trick to use when the house is a mess and you hear visitors coming up the driveway. Run and put the sweeper in the middle of the floor as though you were just beginning to clean. Then you can relax and enjoy the visitor."

9

self it has the 'super, banged-up, lived-in look,'" suggests a Kansas family. "Try to appreciate dolls, story books, toy tractors and colored blocks as part of the decor and beauty of a real home. The house will be neat— maybe too neat—after the children grow up and leave home."

Eventually you'll be able to greet unexpected callers without panic. You won't even apologize for clutter or spilled oatmeal. Besides, the repairman probably left a similar sight and feels right at home.

Get your perspective in focus and set priorities for yourself. Husband is No. 1, then come the children—and then the house, most homemakers agree. "I'm a grandmother now, and believe me, none of the high moments of my life are memories of an impeccable house," writes an Iowa woman.

Of course, you can't ignore the house. Just distinguish between what must be done and what can slide a little. A Washington woman set this minimum standard for herself: Provide the family with simple, nourishing food; clean beds; clean clothes; and a house clean and tidy enough for comfort. Everything else is optional.

Give top billing to things that bug you most when left undone. Your morale may need an orderly porch or a dusted hall. Find out your husband's preferences, too. Something as simple as straightening the contents of the junk drawer might give him the impression you have everything under control.

An Oklahoma woman takes time to bake bread because that makes her husband feel he rates. In Iowa, however, another wife buys baked goods; her husband prefers a neat kitchen to stacks of unwashed bread and cake pans soaking in the sink.

Husbands vary. "You may find the house and your habits don't bother your husband at all—and he may not know that you're upset about not keeping up," says a South Dakota homemaker. "We women often expect our husbands to be mind readers. Tell him how you feel; he may suggest ways to help."

ORGANIZE—THE KEY STEP

"A routine preserves me from self-destruction," states a Florida woman, who voices the opinion of many. "Some people claim a routine gets them down, but the world and everyone in it seems to work on a routine basis—secretaries, doctors, mechanics, even farmers."

A routine is a personal thing. It may be written in detail on paper, especially if you are a "lister." This gives you something to cross off as you complete each job, and you can check your accomplishments at the end of the day. But you also can make an outline in your head. Call it a routine, a schedule, a plan or a guide. The purpose is to give you an

11

idea of what to do when. Whatever your method, keep it flexible, so a sudden change won't wreck your week.

"Check yourself out by keeping a daily record of what you do now. After a few weeks, analyze the record. You'll see how your time is spent and where you should make changes," suggests a Texas woman.

Start a new routine by listing jobs to be done daily, weekly, or monthly, plus extra jobs you want to do. Then assign jobs to days of the week, building around one major "happening" for each day. For instance: Monday, wash; Tuesday, iron; Wednesday, mend; Thursday, wash or catch up; Friday, clean; Saturday, bake; Sunday, church and relax. (This is only an example . . . plans are very personal.) If you have a job outside your home, a daily plan will help you get the most from your at-home time.

Women vary, too. Your own work habits will influence your "happenings." Some women go through the whole house and clean one thing—all the windows or all the rugs; others completely clean one room at a time. Some women wash clothes every day; others do it only once or twice a week, even with an automatic washer and dryer.

Weigh extracurricular jobs. If you enjoy sewing, yard work, gardening, canning and freezing, try to work them in. If you don't like these chores, cut them down to a comfortable size—or cut them out. Don't overspend your energy to save pennies.

Keep these points in mind as you develop your daily plan of things to do:

- Finish one full-attention job and put away the tools before you haul out equipment to start another job. You can vacuum while the washer runs, but you can't vacuum and wax the floors at the same time.
- Do dreaded chores first, then pleasant ones.
- Work at your hours of peak energy. "If you are a morning person, do major jobs early," says a Connecticut wife. "If you are an afternoon person, as I am, save major jobs for late afternoon."
- Try to alternate standing and sitting jobs.
- Keep your plan flexible. Maybe you should take that ride with your husband instead of mopping the floor. And sometimes you may have to clean up spilled paint instead of doing the ironing as planned.

CONSIDER YOURSELF

"A woman can be too unselfish—and lose her identity in her husband or children," says a Missouri wife. "To be worthwhile to one's family, you must first be a worthwhile person to yourself. You need an outlet for creativity, for developing you."

Assign an exclusive piece of each day to yourself—or try the reward principle as a

"I don't think a week has passed in which I have done everything on my schedule, but it is a guide."

South Dakota woman does. Promise yourself a cup of tea, a chat on the telephone or time to sketch as soon as a big chore is done. You might iron six items of clothing, then read one page of a good book. "If you wait until all the work is done, you may not have strength to hold the book," says an avid reader in Iowa.

"I took, and I mean took, a half hour every day for myself," writes a California mother. "I read, sat and looked at the mountains, or napped. It gave me a better perspective on everything."

Other women reserve time to sew, soak in the tub, watch the clouds or jog with their husbands. A daily quiet time to meditate, write letters and count their blessings is a must for many homemakers. For a change of pace, try to leave the house occasionally, if only to window-shop or have your hair done.

Get acquainted with other women. If your neighbors are the older, established kind, use the "ask advice" approach, as a California woman does. Pick something simple like "Have you found a really good floor wax?" Take them a pie or invite them over for coffee. Don't worry about your house. They've probably been through the same struggle and remember it well.

Find at least one woman friend you can really talk with. "Even one telephone call a day can ease the loneliness when you are housebound," says an Iowa homemaker. A

South Dakota woman "talks" by letter to a friend from 4-H camp days. "I can tell her anything. It helps to know she is there 'listening' when my letter arrives."

Your health deserves some attention, too. Make an appointment to visit your doctor for a checkup if you haven't seen him lately. Maybe you need glasses, dentistry, vitamins, iron, more sleep or better-balanced meals. No homemaking routine is going to work if your health is below par.

PUSH A BUTTON

Collect good equipment—vacuum cleaner with attachments, steam iron, rider-mower for a big lawn. All these helpers stretch your energy. You may have to add items one at a time as budget permits, but plan for them.

Most women agree that a dishwasher is their best defense against kitchen clutter. "I've had a dishwasher for years," says a Virginia homemaker, "and I still give it grateful pats when I go by." (Until your dishwasher arrives, try rinsing the dishes, storing them under the sink, then washing them once a day.)

The automatic clothes dryer is another appliance that gets high ratings. "I'd sacrifice buying other things to get a dryer," says an Indiana woman.

LET PEOPLE HELP

Assign the family part of the action. Your husband might lend a hand with heavy mopping and lifting. He also may take a suggestion that he toss his clothes into a handy hamper, even though he's been dropping things in a heap for years. If not, concentrate on his good qualities and train your children to keep the house (which is also theirs) in order.

Part-time help can be a big boost. "When I really get swamped every two or three months, I hire a neighbor girl. She's worth every penny I pay her," writes a 28-year-old Nevada mother of four.

HANG IN THERE

"How many people do you love because they are perfect housekeepers? Probably none. We love people because they are friendly, cheerful, good listeners, interesting and animated—or just plain sweet!"

Old habits aren't easily changed, so don't expect miracles. You can't overhaul yourself, the family and the house all at once. Keep adjusting your work and your plan until things fit. Look for ways to short-cut or improve each job. Borrow ideas from friends, neighbors, Extension bulletins, magazines—and from this very book. Adopt the ideas that work for you; discard others. "There are no hard-and-fast rules to homemaking," says a South Dakota woman. "That's one of the marvelous advantages of the job."

Oh, yes, there will always be a few "down" days, even with the best of plans. Be ready for them. Maybe taking a long walk, changing your hairdo, putting on a special dress or playing a favorite record will perk you up. "Take time to admire what you do accomplish each day, too," urges an Oklahoma woman. Spend an extra minute to look at those sparkling windows, your mouth-watering cake or that freshly ironed shirt.

"Here's how I calm myself when I feel pulled in all directions," writes an Iowa woman. "I look in the mirror. Is this frowning, tight-lipped, tousle-haired bundle of nerves the woman my husband married? For shame! Turn up the corners of your mouth. My, how much better we look and feel when we smile. Then I reach for lipstick and comb so I'll look my best again for the most wonderful man in the world, my husband."

"Our house has tides like the ocean. Each morning debris is carted upstairs, to the front room, the bathroom or clothes hamper. Next morning another tide has rolled in."

House in Order

House in Order

Find a place for everything—
and aim to keep it there

You can dust, scrub and polish all day, yet still have a messy-looking house. Why? Probably because of all that clutter.

It's easy to leave newspapers and books scattered under a table, clean clothes piled on a chair and empty peanut butter jars lined up along the kitchen counter. After you fill all the drawers, cupboards and closets available, the overflow begins to spill out into the rooms. And you have clutter.

That old saying "a place for everything and everything in its place" sounds trite. But it's Survival Rule No. 1 if you want to get your house under control. You need more storage space—or fewer things to store. With determination, you can do something about both parts of the problem.

TOSS OUT THE SURPLUS

Begin by sorting through drawers, closets and cupboards. Dig out old toys, too-small dresses, shoes you haven't worn for a year— and that pan with the broken handle. Don't be sentimental about birthday cards or old school notebooks, either. "Sort on a day when you're a little angry," suggests a Washington State homemaker. "Then you won't be controlled by your heartstrings."

• When you're in doubt about throwing away an old hat, toy or whatever, put it in a special box labeled "Valuable Junk." Allow each family member time to look through and retrieve what he wants before you take the box to the Goodwill store.

■ Keep clutter from accumulating by declaring a Discard Day every so often. Let everyone in the family sort through his own things. Get rid of items you haven't used for some time. The never-used can go to the thrift shop; the once-in-a-while things can go into labeled cardboard cartons.

FIND MORE STORAGE

After you've pared down your possessions a bit, take note of the things that are still cluttering. A South Dakota woman discovered she was always tripping over boots and newspapers, so she added inexpensive storage to get them out of the way.

■ Mount a pegboard panel to the inside of a closet door to provide easy-to-reach storage for umbrellas, purses, gloves, gift wrappings.

■ A chest of drawers installed at the front or back entry is handy if you have school children. When the youngsters come home from school, they can deposit books there until time to do homework. In the morning, they collect their books from the chest without frantic searching. Assign one drawer for extra school supplies, another for boots and rubbers, another for sports equipment.

"I work at neatness as I do being pure in heart. I strive toward it and hope I will be given credit for the effort rather than the result."

21

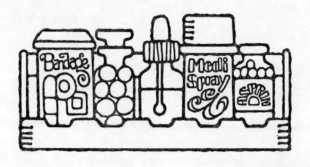

• A small spice rack serves as a downstairs medicine cabinet. Use it to hold aspirin, vitamins, cotton swabs and bandages.

• Attach a bicycle basket to the inside of a closet door to hold scarves and gloves.

• An ironing caddy (the type you can hang over a door) is a good substitute for a guest coat rack near the entry.

• Hinge a step in a stairway that's near the back or side door. Use the space underneath to store boots and rubbers. Also handy for ball bats and catchers' mitts.

• Plastic-coated racks designed to store plates will hold handbags upright on closet shelves.

• A decorated chest in the living room can become a conversation piece. It also can be your emergency catchall for toys and newspapers when unexpected guests arrive.

• If you're lucky enough to have an unused bedroom, turn it into your "Horror Room" where you keep the door closed on mending, ironing, and half-finished projects.

• Removable shelves can be added to any closet or cupboard as needed—without putting nails in the wall. Cut pieces of plywood or wallboard to stand against the side of the closet; then fasten supporting cleats to the boards at the height you want. When shelves are laid in place on the cleats, they hold the plywood sidepieces firmly against the wall.

■ Shoe bags with rows of pockets are great for shoes—but don't overlook their other possibilities. Hang a shoe bag inside the hall closet to hold mittens and gloves. Use another for storing spare light bulbs. On the wall of the recreation room, mount a brightly colored shoe bag for table tennis balls, cards, score pads and game books. In the bedroom, a shoe bag keeps nylon hose sorted and free of snags— or it holds a young collector's treasures of pebbles, dolls, bubble gum wrappers and bottle caps.

Hang a shoe bag in the cleaning closet, too. It separates cleaning cloths. Label each pocket according to contents—wax, furniture polish, window cleaner, etc.

When a plastic shoe bag shows signs of wear, move it to the garage or basement for storing garden tools, seeds, garden shoes and work gloves. Long live the shoe bag!

KITCHEN ADDITIONS

■ Copy the shoe bag, but make just one row of three pockets. Use it for storing plastic bags inside a cabinet. Or make a single pocket of cotton fabric; hang it on the inside of a cabinet door for plastic bowl covers. Run elastic along top edge of the front section so it won't sag.

■Make a rolling pin holder from two spring clamps (used for holding brooms). Screw clamps to the underside of an upper cabinet—near the counter where you bake. Slip the handles of your rolling pin into the clamps.

■Paper bags? Use a dish drainer, a record rack or an honest-to-goodness paper bag holder to keep folded bags in order. A trouser hanger with clips will clamp bags together for hanging in a closet.

■String your measuring spoons on a key chain so they'll be easier to handle. There's more room on a chain than on the original ring.

■Store envelopes of dry soups and salad dressing mixes in a paper napkin holder.

■No place for a paper towel rack? Put a roll of towels inside a deep drawer—at the front. Leave the drawer slightly open and let the edge of the towel stick out.

■An Illinois homemaker attached a holder for paper towels to the underside of her kitchen dining table. It's near her chair, and she finds it handy for mopping up spills at mealtime. She buys pretty bordered towels for that holder, and the family uses them as napkins.

■Save empty foil or waxed paper boxes to use for rolls of shelf paper of the same width. Pull shelf paper out to the length you need; use the cutting edge on the box to tear paper evenly. In other empty cartons, store cords for your small electric appliances. The cartons stack neatly; label them so you can find the cord you want.

■ Fold and roll dish towels before you put them in a drawer. At a glance you can pick up any towel you want without disturbing the others. Drawer stays neat.

■ Knife blades need protection when stored in a drawer. You can make covers with cardboard rolls from waxed paper or foil. Flatten a roll and cut it to fit the knife blade. Fasten one end with staples, masking tape or heavy thread. Or use the white cardboard inserts from nylon stockings or pantyhose packages. Cut two pieces of cardboard to fit the knife blade, then seal the edges with masking tape.

■ A covered cake plate can be left on your kitchen table to hold salt and pepper shakers, sugar bowl and small butter dish—things used at every meal. The cover keeps the small items out of sight and free from dust, and the arrangement saves time and steps.

■ Eliminate kneeling or reaching for pans and food packages inside cupboards that have low, stationary shelves. Place large boxes, set in their lids for reinforcement, on the shelves. The boxes slide forward like drawers.

"The biggest help of all is to put things away. Clutter is harder to deal with than mud."

■Save plastic covers from coffee cans to put on the bottoms of new cans. This protects shelves and counter tops. Empty cans can be decorated and used for storing kitchen tools, crackers, or modeling clay.

■Put magnets to work in the kitchen. Use one inside a kitchen drawer to keep a bottle opener or favorite paring knife in place. Put another on the side of the refrigerator to keep your grocery list within easy reach. Keep a spare magnet on hand to temporarily hold recipes against a metal cabinet—or against another magnet you mount on a wooden cabinet.

■If you need a bulletin board in the kitchen, paint a metal cookie sheet and hang it up. Then use magnets to attach messages, telephone numbers, shopping lists.

■For a space-saving, out-of-sight message center, paint the inside of a cupboard door with blackboard paint. Keep chalk handy.

■Substitute a cup hook for one of the screws when installing a metal towel rack in the kitchen. Use the hook to hang up a vegetable brush or pot holders.

■Keep a list of the hard-to-see contents stored on deep shelves; post it inside the cupboard door. This saves time locating an item. Use a pencil so you can change the list whenever you add or remove something.

■A cup hook mounted near the sink holds rings or bracelets while you prepare food, wash dishes or clean the kitchen floor.

■If you listen to a pocket-size transistor radio in the kitchen, hang it on a cup hook screwed to the underside of a wall cabinet. It's within easy reach and hearing range, but out of harm's way.

■Raise your work counter if it's too low. Simply build a new counter and set it on the low one. Make the new height one that's convenient for you—so you can work with a straight back. Leave the spaces below open; you'll enjoy the extra storage room.

■Use a dish drainer or plate rack for organizing round cake pans and pie plates in a lower cupboard. Some drainers have a silverware compartment that will hold custard cups on their sides. Take another rack for storing heavy cake plates and other special-occasion platters. Plates are protected from chipping, and you can find what you want.

■Use clip-on drapery rings to hang up pot holders. The rings are easy to remove when pot holders go into the laundry hamper.

■A multiple skirt hanger holds several damp dish towels to dry at one time.

■When you need extra counter space, copy an Oregon woman's idea. She pulls out a drawer part way and puts a tray or cookie sheet on it. Wooden chopping board works, too.

▪A large turntable underneath the kitchen sink keeps soaps and cleaners organized.

▪Save a metal TV dinner tray; use it for holding kitchen soap and scouring pads.

▪Hide some carpentry tools in the kitchen. Down in Texas, one husband installed a small spice rack inside a cupboard door—then equipped it with smaller versions of tools his wife kept borrowing from him.

▪Use a bread box that matches your canister set as a kitchen tool chest. This frees a drawer for other things.

▪Put a small shelf on a bracket just outside the back door. Use it to unload groceries while you let yourself in.

▪Keep household keys together by hanging them in a drawer. Use cup hooks screwed to the inside of the front panel. You can put identifying labels on top of the drawer edge.

▪A mirror mounted inside a kitchen cupboard is handy when you want to spruce up for unexpected company—or before a meal.

BATHROOM ORGANIZERS

▪Install a roll of paper towels in the bathroom. Men like them for grimy hands, and guests won't hesitate to use them. They're handy for wiping up spills, too.

■ Organize bathroom essentials on a kitchen-style turntable. Set it on a shelf or counter.

■ A small spice rack can hold individual tumblers for your family.

■ Turn a cobbler's apron into a hair grooming kit. In the large pockets, put curlers, comb, brush and hairnet. Sew on a smaller pocket for bobby pins. Wear the apron while you fix your own hair—or your children's.

■ A magnetic knife holder can organize nail clippers, scissors, nail files and a few pins and needles in your bathroom. Or glue small magnets inside the medicine cabinet to keep these metal items in order.

■ Set a large glass canister filled with toilet soap of different colors in the bathroom. Makes an attractice place to store your extra supply; it's self-serve when a new bar of soap is needed.

■ Coil each end of your bathtub mat toward the center and stand it on end in the tub to drain. If the mat won't stay coiled, snap the rolls together with a clothespin.

■ Keep bathroom scissors from getting lost among the tubes and bottles in your medicine chest. Make a holder from two adhesive bandages. The adhesive sticks to the cabinet, and

"I've noticed that my husband compliments tidiness even more than cleanliness. So I try to pick up and put away as I go along."

29

the gauze section cushions the scissors. Stack the bandages several inches apart on the side wall—or mount them on the underside of a cabinet shelf.

■ You can use cup hooks as individual toothbrush holders. Mount as many as you need.

■ Help your family keep personal articles separated. Ask each person to choose a color. Then his toothbrush, towels, plastic cups, etc., should be of that color.

■ If you have a toothbrush holder, put a plastic teaspoon in it. The spoon, bowl end up, fits nicely into one of the brush slots—handy to the medicine cabinet.

■ Keep four or five extra shower curtain hooks on the rod, inside the shower curtain, to prevent that cluttered look in your bathroom. Use hooks to hang a shower brush, a hot water bottle or hand washables.

■ Make a soap sponge from a bath-size cellulose sponge you buy at the dime store. With a razor blade, cut a pocket in the longest edge of the sponge; insert leftover pieces of soap. Good way to use all the scraps.

■ Keep a supply of small paper cups in the bathroom for use of family and guests. If there's room, mount a special dispenser to hold the cups near the sink.

■ A plastic napkin holder is a handy place to store a bathroom sponge.

■ Spring broom clamps are ideal for safe storage of light bulbs. The clamps come in a variety of sizes. Install some in a bathroom or linen closet. Fasten them to unused wall space or to the underside of a shelf.

■ Copy an Illinois homemaker. Sew a mesh pocket inside the shower curtain to hold soap.

■ Slope the top shelf in your bathroom closet, and place a fairly deep strip of molding along the front edge. Store toilet tissue, soap and facial tissue in vertical rows on this shelf. As the article in front is removed, another will slide down to rest against the molding where you can reach it.

BEDROOM SPACE STRETCHERS

■ Keep small scarves unwrinkled and handy by hanging them in a closet. Attach a strip of rigid foam or sponge to the closet door or wall. Use corsage or hat pins to fasten scarves to the strip.

■ Tack a small pincushion inside your closet to keep a variety of pins handy.

■ Attach a revolving cup hanger to the underside of a closet shelf to hold belts. Or make your own belt holder by screwing cup hooks

31

along the edge of a wooden coat hanger. Or slip shower curtain hooks over your closet rod for hanging belts, purses, umbrellas.

▪ To keep a belt with the dress it matches, mount a cup hook on a wooden coat hanger.

▪ Renew the tightness of a wooden trouser hanger. Glue small pieces of soft sponge to the inner sides of the hanger at each end.

▪ Make a hanger that won't crease trousers, slacks or knit dresses from a wire coat hanger and a cardboard tube. Cut the tube the length of the hanger. With a pair of pliers, cut the bottom wire of the hanger at center. Bend each end away from center to form a half S. Slide the bent wires into the tube ends.

▪ Use pin curl clips to hold low-neckline dresses and blouses on their hangers.

▪ Mount a curtain rod near the bottom of a closet door to use as a simple shoe rack.

▪ Make non-tip hat stands for the closet shelf by re-covering small lampshades.

▪ A convenient hat rack for men can be made for the inside of a closet door. Stretch two wires across the door. Keep them parallel and just far enough apart so the crowns of the hats will fit easily between the wires. Fasten the wires to the door with screw eyes. To insert a hat, slip brim under the wires.

- An old silverware chest, painted to match the bedroom, makes a good jewelry box.

- Keep a magnetic flashlight attached to the metal railing underneath the bed. It's out of sight, yet still handy for emergencies.

- Plastic bags—the big ones for turkeys—are great for storing seldom-used dress shirts and fancy blouses. Keeps them clean.

- To save space, put sweaters in plastic bags and store in the bottom of a garment bag.

- For moth protection, a California homemaker uses a metal tea infuser (the kind for loose tea). She fills it with moth pellets and attaches chain to a clothes hanger in her garment bag.

- If you run out of shelf space for blankets, fold them lengthwise and store them on clothes hangers in a closet. Keep blankets in a zippered garment bag. Or make a cover from a dry cleaning bag.

- Store linens and blankets in seldom-used luggage. Fine for extra bed pillows, too.

- Folded sheets can be quickly identified if you mark T (twin) or F (full) in one corner. Store with that corner up.

- Label shelves in your linen closet to mark location of sheets. On freezer tape, write the sizes—twin, full, queen, king.

"The only time no one drops in is when the house is straight and I've just baked a beautiful cake. If the cake flops, and the sink is full of dishes, and it's been raining all week so the floor is a fright, we have visitors all over the place."

Some Cleaning
Is Necessary

Some Cleaning Is Necessary

*Better a comfortably clean home
than a don't-touch showplace*

You can't live in a house without raising some dust or tracking in dirt. The more children, the more dust-raising and dirt-tracking. Keep that in mind when you buy a new chair, rug, table or sofa pillow. If you want to keep cleaning time to a minimum, choose furnishings that won't need much attention. Before you buy anything for the house, ask yourself: Will it stay clean for a reasonable time? Will it look clean, even when it's soiled? Can it be cleaned—and easily?

Choose such things as stain-resistant fabric finishes for sofas and chairs, and no-iron fabric finishes for curtains. Remember that tweeds and mixtures of colors show soil less than plain, solid colors, whether they appear in furniture or floor coverings.

Find ways to keep the house clean as long as possible. Put mats and foot scrapers at entrances; have boot-parking space by the door. Establish some rules about where youngsters can carry food and drinks. Don't clutter tables with hard-to-dust objects.

TAKE 15 MINUTES A DAY

A tidy house gives the impression that you have a clean house, many homemakers find. To achieve this, they recommend the daily pickup, which takes 10 to 15 minutes. You go through the house, empty ashtrays, collect papers and stray items, clean off flat surfaces and stack magazines. Do this every day. Pick your own time—before you go to bed, while the baby naps or right after breakfast.

One woman lists these three jobs she tackles first every morning: Make the beds, pick up and put away every single thing that's out of place, do dishes and clean the drainboard. You have to decide for yourself what things you will do daily, but set a time limit so you won't drag out the jobs through the whole day.

Beyond your short daily routine, keep flexible. Don't make a ritual out of any household chore. "Some weeks I don't dust upstairs. In winter, I don't always change beds each week," says a Pennsylvania woman. "In other words, I never let habit alone drive me to do something. I look for ways to cut down on the work."

TOOLS TO EASE IT

- For daily pickups, carry a large paper bag with you. Into it, empty ashtrays and wastebaskets. It saves trips back and forth to the trash container. Or wheel your laundry cart through the house as you straighten up. The cart serves as a delivery wagon for out-of-place toys, books or clothing.

- Use a dust mop in place of a broom, and you get the dirt and dust all at once. Better yet, use a vacuum to pick up all the dirt.

"I've found everyone else's house usually looks cleaner than mine, just because it's different dirt."

■ Before you dust or vacuum, tape a small paper bag to your apron or belt. In it, you can drop stray bobby pins, crayons and pencils you find along the way.

■ Make yourself a cleaning apron with big pockets. Use one pocket to carry your dust mitt and another to collect stray items.

■ Take a cotton-tipped swab stick to wipe dust and oil smudges from the hard-to-reach number plate under the telephone dial.

■ Borrow the long-handled snow brush from the car to clean out narrow, hard-to-reach places. A discarded child's broom is good for cleaning crevices, too.

■ To clean or paint behind radiators or other hard-to-reach places, tack a 3"-square sponge to the end of a yardstick. Dip sponge in cleaner or paint and manipulate it with the yardstick handle.

■ When washing walls, woodwork or windows, wrap a washcloth, a rag or a 3" strip of absorbent cotton around your working wrist. Hold the fabric or cotton in place with rubber bands, so it catches any dirty water that might drip down your arm.

■ Remove lint and dust from beneath the refrigerator or any very narrow place with a "dust mop" made from a yardstick that has an old nylon stocking over it.

■ When the baby outgrows his soft-bristle hair brush, use it to dust your sheer fabric lamp shades. The fine bristles will not injure delicate fabrics.

■ A New Jersey mother says her daughter's play carpet sweeper just fits the stair treads. She uses it for quick pickups.

■ Speed your dusting chores by using both hands. Take two old socks (they don't have to match), slip one on each hand and go to work.

■ A Kentucky homemaker says a soft paint brush is the handiest tool in her cleaning kit. She likes it for dusting lampshades, picture frames and hard-to-reach places. She uses it damp or dry and says the brush itself is easy to clean. (A 1″ paint brush is great for dusting louvered doors.)

■ Slip the heads of oiled or dirty mops into plastic bags before storing so they won't soil the walls or floors.

■ Cover the lower part of your mop handle by winding a length of 2″ velvet ribbon around it. This keeps handle from marring furniture you are dusting under.

■ Mark your scrub pail into quart measures with red nail polish. Makes it easy to mix cleaning solutions the proper strength. (If you have a plastic pail, test a spot to be sure the polish won't damage it.)

■ Exposed bed springs may be cleaned by using a damp, long-handled dish sponge.

■ Buy large-size cellulose sponges, then cut them into smaller sizes and shapes you need for particular jobs.

■ A round pastry brush is a good size for cleaning out the lint filter on some automatic clothes dryers.

■ Slide a piece of rubber hose over the handle of your work pail. When the pail is full, it's easier to carry.

■ Make a quickie cobbler's apron to protect you on dirty jobs. Take a plastic bag, such as dry cleaners use, and cut out holes for your neck and arms.

■ Prolong the life of rubber or plastic gloves. Turn them wrong side out and put a piece of adhesive tape over the end of the first and second fingers (the ones that show wear quickest). When you wear the gloves right side out, your fingernails rub the tape, instead of the glove.

■ Rubber or plastic gloves will slip off easily if you hold your gloved hands in cold water for a few seconds. You can feel gloves loosen as your hands cool off.

■ Work gloves (plastic, rubber or cotton) still have some use after one wears out. Usually, the right-hand glove goes first. Take two left-hand gloves, turn one inside out to make a new "pair." These are fine for dirty jobs.

■ When the liquid in a spray bottle of window cleaner gets low, cut a piece from a drinking straw and use it as an extension on the sprayer tube. It works fine—lets you use the last bit of cleaner in the bottle.

■ To protect wallpaper when washing or waxing baseboards, hold a 12″ plastic ruler or piece of heavy cardboard along the top of the baseboard as you work.

■ Use a plastic windshield scraper to remove flour from a pastry board or for other scraping jobs in the kitchen.

■ Let a small utility cart help you wash windows. Set equipment on the cart; wheel the cart from window to window and from room to room. There are no wet rings on the floor, and you avoid a lot of stooping.

■ Put scratch-remover furniture polish in a thoroughly washed shoe polish bottle. The dauber that comes in the bottle is handy for applying polish to scratches.

■ Stitch two thicknesses of nylon net to your dishcloth. You'll have a soft and rough side in your hand at all times—speeds any dishwashing you do by hand.

"Invite some company over, even if you have no idea how you will get ready for them. This seems to be the extra push we need to get at digging out the corners."

41

■ Use kitchen tongs to grasp the dishcloth when you clean the inside of tall jars.

■ Save an empty detergent bottle with a dispenser cap to use for self-polishing floor wax. You can pour the right amount of wax on the floor—easier than pouring each time from a heavy gallon container.

■ A floor polisher can be made from a worn-out toilet lid cover. Slip cover over a dust mop; pull drawstring tight and tie in place.

■ A clothes-sprinkler cap on a bottle of furniture polish will spread polish evenly over a dust mop or dustcloth.

■ After defrosting a chest freezer, use a sponge mop to soak up any water left in the bottom. Saves stooping and helps get water out of hard-to-reach corners.

■ For some jobs, you can cut steel wool soap pads into four pieces. Use one piece for a single job, then discard it.

HANDY HOW-TO'S

■ Use shelf paper or newspaper to cover the tops of kitchen cupboards that do not reach all the way to the ceiling. The paper need not show, and you can dispose of the greasy dirt that collects, simply by changing the paper. This is easier than climbing up on a ladder with pail and sponge to scrub.

■ A California homemaker recommends giving all game boards, such as checkerboards, two coats of colorless shellac before they are used. This makes the boards easy to wipe clean and helps them last longer.

■ Drain silverware in a colander when washing dishes. Silver dries quickly after scalding, can't fall through the colander as it does through some dish racks.

■ Line the shelves of your metal cabinets with self-adhesive plastic. It will last for years and cannot slide.

■ Stop dust, crumbs and grease from getting into the tiny spaces between counters and counter-height appliances in your kitchen. Cover the crack with a strip of freezer tape. Or use plastic tape in a matching color.

■ Wax windowsills and sashes so they will be easier to dust.

■ Save washing out wastebaskets and garbage cans. Set the waste container on folded newspapers (many thicknesses). Draw around it and cut out the papers, leaving a tab on one side for easy lifting. Put the pad of paper in the bottom of container; remove sheets as they become soiled.

■ Cut several shelf liners at one time, then layer them. When the top layer is soiled, remove it and use the next layer.

■ Prevent drips and marks on refrigerator shelves by slipping soft plastic bowl covers on the bottoms of milk cartons—or set the cartons in rigid plastic food containers.

■ After the meal is over, try to wash the silverware right away. At least rinse off forks and other pieces used for foods that cause tarnish —eggs, salt, mayonnaise.

■ Don't put rubber bands in your silverware chest. Rubber causes tarnishing.

■ When you hand-wash delicate china or glassware, spread a clean towel in the bottom of the sink or pan. This provides a cushion and helps prevent chipping.

■ How do you prevent a build-up of wax on your kitchen floors? Don't wax within 6" of a baseboard—at least after the first application. There's no traffic to wear off layers you apply close to the wall.

■ Speed up the drying of a freshly waxed floor. Put an oscillating fan where it can blow over the surface.

■ Glue pieces of felt to the bottom of chair and table legs to keep them from marking newly waxed kitchen floor coverings.

■ When cleaning a bathroom cupboard above a washbasin, lay a pastry board across the basin to hold items removed from the shelves.

- To clean under some dressers, take out the bottom drawer and insert the nozzle of your vacuum attachment in the opening. You won't damage the floor, the carpet or your back from moving this heavy furniture.

- Let the automatic clothes dryer fluff and remove dust from shag rugs, chenille spreads, bed and sofa pillows. Tumble draperies for a few minutes to freshen them.

- Time yourself on cleaning jobs. When you have 5, 10 or 15 minutes to spare, you know which job you can handle. Maybe you can straighten out the junk drawer, polish a candleholder or clean a mirror.

CLEANING TRICKS

- Make your own solution for cleaning wood-paneled walls that are finished with varnish or a sealer. Mix ½ cup pure gum turpentine, 1 cup boiled linseed oil (you buy it boiled at the hardware store, and 1 tablespoon vinegar. Apply a thin coat and rub gently with a soft cloth. Polish with a dry cloth.

- To dust papered walls, use a soft brush or cloth. Or make a soft fabric cover for your broom. Begin dusting at the top of the wall and work down. Use very light, even strokes. If the brush or cloth becomes soiled, change to a clean one.

"For serious cleaning, I wait until I get an irresistible urge. A woman can do four days' work in a few hours during a 'scrub seizure.'"

■ If children have scribbled on the wallpaper with wax crayon, an Illinois homemaker suggests using fine steel wool to remove the markings. She finds they disappear with little damage done.

■ Wear cotton gloves when you dust, wash or wax Venetian blinds at the window. Use both hands to speed the job. For washing, dip your gloved hands into a pail of thick suds and squeeze out excess moisture; the gloves become your cleaning cloths.

■ You can use either a wax or a polish to help clean and protect wood furniture that is finished with varnish, lacquer or a penetrating seal. Whichever you decide to use, stick with it. The job will be easier and your furniture will look better than if you keep switching between the two methods of care.

■ To wash a fabric lampshade, be sure the fabric is sewn to the frame, not glued. Remove any excess trim, then dip the shade up and down in a washtub or bathtub of thick, sudsy (mild) water. Rinse with a clean water dip. Hang the shade from a clothesline or rod to dry. You can use an electric fan to help speed the drying time.

■ Clean steel cabinets with the same wax recommended for use on refrigerators and other appliances. It cleans and protects the finish in one operation.

■Remove lime deposits from your teakettle with three parts water and one part vinegar. Bring to a boil and let stand overnight. Discard the solution and wash the kettle.

■Quick way to clean tarnished silverware is with the electrolytic method. Take an aluminum pan or an enamel pan with a sheet of aluminum foil spread over the bottom. Add enough water to cover the silver. For each quart of water, use 1 teaspoon of salt and 1 teaspoon of baking soda. Bring the solution to a boil. Add the silver and boil for 2 or 3 minutes until tarnish has disappeared. Remove silver with tongs; wash in hot sudsy water. Rinse and dry. *Caution:* Do not use the electrolytic method on silver that has a shaded, ornate pattern—the method will lighten the entire pattern. And don't use the method on knives with hollow handles. Incidentally, the aluminum foil or the pan will darken in this process—so don't use your best aluminum pan for the job.

■You can brighten an aluminum cooking pan that's gotten dull. Cook an acid food, such as tomatoes or rhubarb in the pan. (Eat the food, of course. It's fine.)

Or boil a solution of 2 teaspoons of cream of tartar (or 1 tablespoon of vinegar) to 1 quart of water in the pan until discoloration is removed. Finish brightening the pan by scouring it with a soap pad of steel wool.

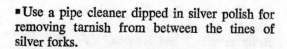

- Use a pipe cleaner dipped in silver polish for removing tarnish from between the tines of silver forks.

- If you have a clean-it-yourself oven, here's a way to take care of grease spatters. Fill a small bowl with household ammonia and set it in the cool oven. Close the door and leave overnight. This helps loosen the grease and makes cleaning easier.

For burned-on grease spots, moisten a cloth (such as an old washcloth) with household ammonia and leave it on the spot for an hour or so. Then wash the spot away. (Keep ammonia off aluminum parts.)

- Remove stuck-on food from pots and pans by adding a small amount of water. Bring the water to a boil, remove from heat, cool and wash as usual.

- Want a homemade cleaner for brass and copper? Sprinkle on salt and a little vinegar. Rub, rinse and dry. You'll find a plastic squeeze bottle is an ideal container for keeping this mixture handy to the sink.

- To wipe out your refrigerator, use a solution of 1 or 2 tablespoons of baking soda dissolved in a quart of warm water.

- Tea or coffee stains on china often can't be washed off. No problem. Make a paste of baking soda and water and rub stains away.

"My living room always looked as if it needed cleaning—until I realized dust on the big piano made the whole room look dirty. Now I give the piano a lick and a promise at least once a day."

- To remove stains from plastic cups, use chlorine bleach solution. Directions on the container tell you how.

- An art gum eraser or wallpaper cleaner (dough-type) will take off some smudges from non-washable window shades.

- You can dust windows with soft tissue paper.

- Homemade window-washing solution is 2 tablespoons of ammonia to a quart of warm water. Another is 2 tablespoons of vinegar to a quart of warm water. Don't spatter the woodwork as you wash.

- When you wash windows, rub from side to side on the inside of the glass, up and down on the outside. If there are any streaks, you can tell which side they are on.

- Clean a plaster cast on a broken arm or leg with white shoe polish.

- When washing walls, begin at the bottom and work up. If water drips down over a clean area, you can easily wipe it away. But when water drips down over a soiled area, you have streaks that often are difficult to remove. Sounds crazy, but it's true.

"In each room have a pretty spot that is dusted and arranged to delight the eye of the beholder."

Fixing Up

Fixing Up

A little glue, plaster and paint
helps keep the house in good shape

Why can't a house and furniture stay new-looking forever? Wishful thinking! From the first day someone sits on your new sofa or chair, the furniture begins to develop a lived-in look. And no matter how careful everyone is, the walls are going to get bumps and scratches.

There are ways to slow down the aging process, of course. You can protect furnishings and do minor repairs when they are first needed, to make things last longer. Later, there are ways to give used furnishings a second go-round. When it's finally time to redecorate, perhaps a change of color and a few new furnishings will perk up you, as well as the house.

FURNITURE

■ Don't let candlesticks or bookends scratch tables. Cut pieces of moleskin or special adhesive flannel to fit bottoms of these objects. Peel the backing off the material and press it in place. Or cut a piece of sponge rubber, ⅛" thick, and hold it in place with rubber cement. You'll also find packages of ready-to-use protectors of self-adhesive flannel, cork or plastic.

■ Make a work cover for your dining room table from heavy, fabric-backed vinyl. Fit it like a card table cover, with strong elastic across the corners to hold it in place. Cover protects table from scratches of scissors or pins and from dabs of the children's paints.

▪ To keep a sofa or heavy chair from sliding on a smooth surface, glue small pieces of foam rubber to the bottom of the legs. This keeps the furniture from leaving marks on the floor and also from hitting the wall.

▪ An Iowa woman put two spring-type door stops (3″ long) on her sofa. She screwed them into the lower back of the sofa frame. The cushioned knobs rest against the wall, and they protect both sofa and wall.

▪ Glue felt weather stripping to the underside of rockers on a chair. This eliminates marred floors and muffles the noise.

▪ Turn a discarded high chair to new uses. It will make (A) a child-height chair (rungs added to support shortened legs); (B) a standing bed tray (from swing-back tray nailed to arm supports); (C) a small shelf (from foot rest); (D) a kitchen stool, with or without a back. If you make the child's chair (A), add a top to the cut-off leg ends and you have (E) a child's play table.

▪ A Kansas woman made a highboy from two old dressers bought at a sale. (You often can get good buys—without mirrors—at auctions and junk shops.) She removed the legs and

"A new house may be handier than an old one, but it still needs attention. And oh, how the scratches show! I almost had a nervous breakdown trying to keep mine 'new.'"

53

mirror supports, then securely fastened one chest on top of the other. After a coat of paint and new drawer pulls, she found the cost of the six-drawer chest totaled $3.

■ Make a tourniquet to tighten a newly glued chair round. To glue: Scrape old glue from the ends and sockets and apply a reliable glue mixed with a little sawdust. Let glue set a few minutes; press ends of the round into the chair leg sockets. Then tie rope or sturdy cloth around the two chair legs. Place a small stick through center of the loop and turn stick to twist rope tight. Wipe away excess glue. Prop stick against chair round to hold the rope firm. Leave overnight or until glue is dry.

■ Use plastic wood to take the wobble out of a chair that has one leg shorter than the others. Place a lump of plastic wood on a piece of paper on the floor; press the short leg down onto the plastic wood until the chair is level. Scrape away the excess; let the plastic wood dry and sand smooth.

■ Fit the top cover for a studio couch like a contour sheet. Cover stays in place and is easy to take off to wash.

■ When using plastic to cover chairs, you will get a smoother, tighter fit if the plastic is warm when you start working. It's also easier to handle. Place plastic near a heater or in a window for the sun to warm.

■ Space decorative tacks evenly when you re-upholster furniture. With transparent or masking tape, fasten a tape measure on the fabric along the line where tacks will be placed. The tape measure helps you space tacks at regular intervals.

■ Protect upholstered furniture from soil with back and arm mats of the same upholstery material. Ask the store to order extra fabric for this purpose. Matching covers look better and give more protection than the old-fashioned crocheted doilies.

■ Slipcovers won't slip or slide out of shape if you buy rubber kneeling pads, cut them in half lengthwise, and insert them in the tuck-in space around the seat cushions.

■ When putting loose knobs back on dresser drawers, dip the screws into a little clear shellac or fingernail polish before resetting them. They'll turn more easily. The shellac (or nail polish) will retard rusting—and when it hardens, those screws will be set.

FLOORS AND RUGS

■ To align stair treads, determine the exact location of treads at top and bottom of stairway and mark the places with tacks. Then tie lengths of string between the sets of tacks. Install treads, aligning edges of treads with the strings.

■ To remove cracked or worn asphalt tile, cover it with a sheet of paper and heat it with your hot electric hand iron. Heat softens the adhesive on the back, and tile comes out more easily.

■ Toys and small objects can't drop through the furnace registers in your floors if you wire a piece of window screen to the underside of the grating.

■ Cut linoleum or vinyl floor covering to fit around odd-shaped corners by using a guide made from paper—or use a length of pliable solder. Press solder against baseboard or projection until it conforms to the shape. Trace shape on floor covering and cut.

■ If your rugs aren't nailed in place, turn them around once or twice a year. This distributes wear and adds to the overall life of the rugs.

■ Kitchen-style turntables protect the carpeting under large houseplants. These underliners also make it easy to rotate the plants toward the light so they grow more evenly.

WALLS

■ A large sheet of pegboard can be the background for a group of family photographs, mounted in simple, inexpensive frames. The pegboard lets you rearrange or change pictures without putting nails in the wall. Hang the pegboard in a hallway, kitchen or corner of the family room.

▪ To save the bedroom walls from her teen-age daughter's "pin-up-itis," an Idaho woman made a bulletin board of heavy cardboard (about 1″ thick). This was mounted in a large picture frame that had a fresh coat of gold paint. The bulletin board displays pictures and school notes.

▪ An Oregon mother encouraged her teen-age son to confine his school pennants and clippings to the pegboard paneling that covers half a wall in his bedroom.

▪ Arrange snapshots behind glass in one large picture frame lined with black fabric. Change the snaps frequently to keep them up-to-date and interesting.

▪ To hold pictures straight on the wall, tape a thumbtack to the back of the picture near the bottom. Head of the tack should be against the picture, with the point protruding through the tape. When picture is in place, press point of tack into wall.

▪ To hold frames away from the wall and prevent hard-to-remove dark streaks from forming along the bottom, stick bunion plasters behind the lower corners of large pictures, corn plasters behind small pictures.

"When mending wallpaper, tear the paper instead of cutting it. Torn edges blend in with the design better than straight edges, and your patch will scarcely be noticeable."

■ To find light switches in the dark, put a dot of luminous paint or a strip of luminous tape on light switches. You can see the glow in the dark.

■ Plaster cracks can be painted out of existence with a paintbrush and a dish of patching plaster mixed with water to the thickness of heavy paint.

Tint patching plaster with food coloring or dye to match the color of your wall. Fill small holes or cracks to save redecorating the whole wall.

■ Before repapering a wall, insert pieces of matchstick in the holes left when you moved shelves or whatnots. Cut the sticks just long enough so you can feel them under the new paper. Saves time, temper and wall finish when you rehang the shelves; the matchsticks also will tend to tighten the screws or nails in the old holes.

■ Apply a coat of clear nail polish or clear shellac over any grease spots before hanging new wallpaper. Grease will not soak through.

■ Use a floor sponge mop to soak wallpaper before removing it. With mop, you can use very hot water. Takes less effort to reach the top of the wall. Or use a paint roller dipped in hot water to moisten paper until it can be scraped off.

■ Use your electric mixer to blend wallpaper paste to lump-free smoothness. Wash mixer thoroughly afterward.

■ An Iowa woman recommends using a cup of vinegar to a pail (10 quarts) of water to soak old wallpaper for removal. She finds it hastens the job.

■ Apply wallpaper paste with a paint roller—spreads paste evenly, is quicker and reduces spattering.

■ Before papering a ceiling, make a holder by fastening a strip of wood (wider than the paper) to a long handle. Then your helper can raise each strip of paste-covered paper up to you as you stand on a ladder. Ends of paper are folded over (but not creased) so paper doesn't slide off frame or dangle down and get torn. You won't have to support full weight of long strip while putting up paper. Helps make a neater job.

■ Save leftover wallpaper for patching. Use extra to cover wastebaskets or file boxes.

DOORS AND WINDOWS

■ Modernize an old-fashioned door by covering it with a sheet of ¼" plywood or prefinished paneling. Attach with glue or headless nails. You can complete the transformation by adding a new doorknob.

■ To oil the lock on your door quickly and easily, dip the key in oil and turn it in the lock several times. This accomplishes the oiling with little mess and effort.

■ If you find it difficult to turn your key in a lock, try some lubricating graphite to loosen it. Graphite comes in a puff-type plastic container and is sold at hardware and variety stores. Squirt a few puffs into the lock, then turn the key several times to lubricate lock.

■ Protect a windowsill with self-adhesive plastic so a plant or bouquet won't mar it. You won't have to worry about scaly paint, and the sill is easy to clean.

Some homemakers install ceramic tile on windowsills to give this same protection.

■ For tieback curtains, stick adhesive-backed picture hooks to the edges of the window casing. Slip tiebacks over the hooks. No need to damage the wall or casing with nails.

■ Draperies you've just made—or ones you've had cleaned—can be coaxed to hang in perfect folds. Put draperies on rods, and pull rods open. Pin in the pleats at the bottom of each panel to match the pleats at the top; leave pinned until pleats fall into shape.

You also can shape the pleats by tying cords around the opened draperies. With pleats in place, tie one cord around the fabric, just above the hemline. Tie another halfway between hemline and top of drapery.

▪ A Michigan woman disguised exposed drapery rods with wood-grained self-adhesive paper that blends with her wall paneling.

▪ When you put curtains on small rods, slip a thimble over the end of the rod. The curtain slips on in a second and no threads are pulled. Or try covering the end of the rod with a finger cut from an old glove. Saves time, temper and the curtain.

▪ Make a "frosted" window for bathroom privacy with white opaque plastic. Apply plastic with thick starch or wallpaper paste, or use self-adhesive material.

▪ Line matchstick bamboo curtains or blinds with fabric to match your color scheme. Lining provides greater privacy at night, and it looks more attractive by day.

▪ To wind up the spring in a window shade, insert flat end of the roller in the narrow slot of a keyhole. Turn the other end of the roller until the spring is tight.

▪ To open a window that sticks, work from the outside. Shove a putty knife under the window sash below the side rail; then insert another putty knife under the first one. Put the metal tip of a screwdriver between the two putty knife blades and gently tap the end of screw-

"Some organization is necessary, but maybe you are spending too much time listing *and not* enough doing."

61

driver handle. This releases the window without marring paint.

KITCHENS

▪ Give new life to old steel or wood cabinets by covering the fronts with self-adhesive plastic cut to fit drawers and doors. For a neat job, remove handles before you apply the plastic, then replace them.

▪ Cover the bottom of metal wastebaskets with moistureproof self-adhesive plastic to help prevent rust.

▪ Line kitchen shelves and drawers with plastic shelf liner in white or a color. Or use clear plastic carpet protector you buy by the yard. Materials are easy to cut and easy to clean.

▪ If you have a corner sink with no view, copy the idea of a Wisconsin homemaker. She pins up a pretty landscape picture and changes it occasionally. Sometimes she adds a poem that she commits to memory as she cleans vegetables or washes dishes.

▪ A Michigan woman discovered she couldn't see the words "on" and "off" on her electric range when she was across the room. She put red nail polish at the "off" marking on each disk. Then she could tell at a glance when a unit was turned on.

■ Bookends in a Kentucky kitchen are two cans of fruit with attractive labels. The homemaker used them as a temporary measure to prop up her cookbooks, but received so many compliments she never replaced the idea. (She does change the cans occasionally so contents won't get too old.)

■ Rubber washers glued to the bottom of a metal bread box will allow air to circulate underneath so the box won't rust.

■ Use a large cork to replace a broken knob on a pot lid. Push a sharp screw up through the hole, and twist the cork onto it. Cork makes a heatproof knob.

■ Match table coverings to the kitchen wall by making easy-to-clean place mats from leftover wallpaper. Cover the mats with clear, self-adhesive plastic.

OUTDOOR AREAS

■ Protect porch pillows from dampness by using a plastic slipcover under the regular pillow covering.

■ Paint the edge of the bottom step of your outside entrance white—it's easier to see in dim light.

■ If you have a roadside mailbox, use reflector tape to spell out letters of your name so it can be read easily at night.

■ Use an outdoor-type double-socket fixture with two bulbs for a yard light that is hard to reach. When one bulb burns out, you still have light until the dead bulb can be replaced. Always install two new bulbs. You can use the older bulb in a more accessible place.

■ Paint luminous strips in your garage as guides for parking.

■ An old ice skate blade nailed upside down on the doorstep helps scrape mud and snow off boots.

■ If your front porch is slippery in rainy or snowy weather, apply some non-slip bathtub strips.

■ Use a hose-type signal bell (the kind gas stations have) for your driveway. The bell can be in your house so you're alerted when visitors come.

■ If you have empty outdoor light sockets, keep them clean, dry and shockproof by inserting burned-out fuses.

WITH PAINT

■ Turn an unopened paint can upside down for 24 hours or so before beginning to work. The paint will mix more easily, especially if it has been standing awhile since you purchased it. Be sure the lid is on tight before upending the can.

■ When you paint, protect floors and other surfaces by gluing a paper plate to the bottom of the paint can. This makes a handy place to rest your paintbrush, too.

■ When you paint a ceiling, wear a clear plastic rain bonnet pulled forward over your eyes. Keeps paint off hair, face and glasses, yet lets you see your work.

■ Put a strong rubber band lengthwise around your paint can—so the band makes a "bridge" across the top. Use the band to wipe excess paint off brush as you work.

■ Old plastic draperies, tablecloths and shower curtains make good drop cloths. You can staple several pieces together to make an extra large drop cloth.

■ Move your picnic table indoors to stand on when you paint or wash ceilings. Table is easier to move than sawhorses and planks, and it provides plenty of room for paint or cleaning supplies. You can do a larger area at one time than when you use a ladder.

■ When finished painting, brush a strip on the outside of your paint can to indicate the level of what's inside. You'll know not only the color, but also how much paint you have left.

■ Worn plastic bowl scrapers are fine for mixing paint and for getting the last bit of paint from the can.

■ Use a plastic shower cap to protect your hair from paint spatters.

■ Pre-treat a new paintbrush to be used for oil-base paints by suspending it in linseed oil for 12 hours before using. Make sure bristles do not rest on can bottom. Brush will be easier to clean, as oil paint or enamel sticks to untreated bristles.

■ Keep paintbrush bristles straight when soaking in turpentine. Run a stiff wire (coat hanger wire is fine) through a hole bored in the brush handle; rest wire across the rim of a can containing turpentine. Drill the hole low enough for the suspended brush to clear can bottom where the paint settles.

■ To suspend a paintbrush in cleaning solution, cut crisscross slots in the plastic top of a coffee can and poke the handle of the brush through from underneath. The plastic will grip the handle of the brush and suspend it; the lid retards evaporation.

■ When painting a pipe, protect the wall, ceiling or floor that the pipe runs through with a collar of waxed paper or aluminum foil. Fold the paper or foil into quarters and cut out folded center tip to make a circle the size of the pipe. Slit paper so that you can slip collar around the pipe, and tape it to the surface you want to protect.

■A piece of rough carpet, tacked on the end of a block of wood, makes a good "brush" to paint wire screening. Dip carpeted end of block in paint and rub across the screen—it won't splash.

■Paint a bowl or tray on both sides without waiting for one side to dry. Paint the bottom (or outside) first. Make a "rack" by pushing four thumbtacks up through a large piece of cardboard, and rest the bowl (or tray) on the points of the tacks while you paint the inside. You can place tape over the heads of the thumbtacks so they will stay in place if the cardboard is moved.

■When you paint a picture frame, tack a thin strip of wood across the back. Use the strip as a handhold.

■For steps that must be used daily, you can paint half of each step and let it dry thoroughly. Then paint the other half. As a reminder of fresh paint, stretch a rope down the middle of the steps. The rope will not mar the paint and will remind everyone to use the dry side.

Or you can paint every other step. Then put strips of paper (held in place by masking tape) on unpainted steps to guide family members going up and down the stairs. When paint is dry, switch paper strips to finished steps and complete the job.

■ Use an empty bottle with brush (such as a nail polish bottle) for storing some leftover paint. You have the exact color for minor repair work, and the small brush is handy for touching up chips and scratches.

■ When painting a chair or stool, drive a nail in the bottom of each leg. Use 2″ nails and drive them in only ½″. This will do away with collars of excess paint around the bottom of the legs.

■ Use auto touch-up paint or spray-can enamel to match colors of heating registers to your new carpeting.

TOOLS TO HELP

■ If you can't stick enameled thumbtacks in hard wood with your thumb, cover a hammer head with adhesive tape; then drive in the tack. Protects the enameled finish, so thumbtacks won't be chipped.

■ No finger smashing is necessary to drive tacks in out-of-the-way places. Stick them through light cardboard, hammer in, then pull the cardboard loose.

■ For big sandpapering jobs on uneven surfaces, cut two pieces of sandpaper into the rough shape of a mitten (no thumb) to fit your hand. Fasten edges together with masking tape. When one side becomes too smooth to do a good job, turn it over and use the other side. Wear a glove to insulate your hand against heat from friction.

▪ When a repair job involves small parts, screws, nails, or tacks, keep these easy-to-lose items in order by sticking them to a strip of masking tape.

▪ You can make a plaster-patching tool by taping a beverage can opener lengthwise to the handle of a paintbrush. Use the opener to cut out loose plaster, and the brush to wet edges of the crack before you fill it with the patching plaster.

▪ Make a rim around the platform at the top of your stepladder by attaching quarter-round molding along each edge. Tools, pail or a can of nails will stay put when you are working.

▪ Use a discarded lunch box to organize the tools you need most frequently for jobs around the house.

▪ To make sure everyone returns household tools they borrow, hang tools on a board in your utility room. Outline the shape of the hammer, pliers, screwdriver, etc. If you feel artistic, you might draw a picture incorporating tool shapes. (The hammer could be part of a long, low sports car, for instance, and the pliers, a slim driver.) You can tell at a glance if a tool is missing.

"Go sit down for 10 minutes every once in a while. Think about what you want to do the rest of the day. Rock the baby, read a short article or just relax. But set the timer—so you won't stay too long."

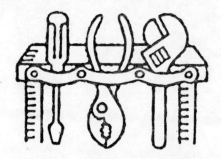

■Make loops with a leather strap at the top of your stepladder to hold pliers, hammer, screwdriver or other tools you might need for repair jobs. This will save making trips up and down the ladder.

■Slip fingertips that are cut from old leather gloves over the jaws of pliers when handling polished metal. This helps avoid scratches, and it takes less time than wrapping the metal with tape.

■Handy tool for any home is a ¼"-capacity electric drill. Use it whenever you hang anything on the wall—even a tiny picture. The drill cuts a clean hole through plaster and eliminates the chipping you get with a hammer and nail. (Sometimes, covering the spot first with crossed strips of transparent tape helps avoid the nail-hammer chipping—but don't count on it.)

■When refinishing wood furniture, use a nut pick to remove softened paint or varnish from carvings or grooves. Slide a piece of string back and forth in the turned grooves on chair rungs or legs.

■After repairing a small broken object with glue, place glued part between the jaws of a pair of pliers; put a rubber band around the handles to hold jaws firm. Pliers act as a small vise to hold repairs steady until the glue has time to dry.

■ Don't improvise a platform with chairs and stools when you climb up to hang curtains or wash windows. Nothing works as well—or as safely—as a sturdy stepladder.

■ A spray-top bottle filled with turpentine is handy in the workshop. A squirt or two makes it easy to clean paint or grease from your hands and arms.

LITTLE INGENUITIES

■ Favorite vase or flower bowl cracked? Coat the inside with a layer of paraffin, and let it harden. Coating lasts indefinitely, and vase (or bowl) won't leak.

■ Paper drawer liners stay in place if you first cut a piece of cardboard to fit the bottom of the drawer. Cut paper liners an inch larger all around and fold excess under the edge of the cardboard. Hold edges in place with masking tape.

■ Large pieces of self-adhesive paper are easier to work with if they are chilled in the refrigerator for a half hour. (Cut the paper to the desired size and shape before placing in the refrigerator.) When the backing is removed, the gummed surface remains dry and non-sticky for a few minutes, giving you time to get it in position. At room temperature, the paper soon regains its adherent quality.

▪Remove only an inch of the protective backing from the edges of self-adhesive paper when you line a shelf or drawer. Liners stay in place just as well and are easier to remove when you need replacements.

▪Replace all bulbs in a multilight ceiling fixture when one bulb burns out—the others soon will burn out, too. You'll need a ladder less often than if you replace bulbs one at a time. Any still-good bulbs can be used for table lamps, which are much easier to change.

▪Plastic thread raveled from a plastic pot cleaner is fine for mending or tying jobs that need very strong string. Heat will melt the plastic, so don't use it near a flame or hot iron.

▪Fireplace screens can be given a new look with black liquid shoe polish.

▪Perk up the inside of an old medicine cabinet with adhesive-backed plastic. It comes in many colors and designs, it's easy to apply and it's waterproof.

▪Improve the overhead view for the occupant of a lower bunk by covering slats of the upper bunk with a piece of heavy cardboard. This can be cut from a large carton, such as the one a refrigerator comes in. Use paint or paper to decorate it.

"You wouldn't think of starting a job in town in an old ragged outfit and uncombed hair, would you? Don't start at home that way, either. Only difference—at home wear comfortable shoes."

72

■ Next time you change the fluorescent tubes in the bathroom, check the type you're using. Replace them with warm white deluxe tubes. Fluorescent lamps affect colors in a room— and in your skin. Cool white tends to make you look a bit blue. Warm white (deluxe, please) is closest to incandescent light. It will make you feel better about yourself when you look in the mirror.

"A stack of dirty dishes is not a sign of a neglected house. It's just a sign that people like to eat."

Everybody Eats

Everybody Eats

Make kitchen chores routine,
but let the meals sparkle

You probably spend more working time in your kitchen than in any other room of the house. Cooking food, preparing snacks, serving meals, washing dishes, cleaning up. Two or three times a day. It's a big part of any homemaker's life.

You may be a gourmet cook and like to make everything from scratch. But a family with hungry children will force you to whip out some quickie meals, too. Why not adopt ideas to cut your time in the kitchen, especially chore time, to a minimum? Save those extra minutes to spend on something more creative—sewing, reading, or perhaps preparing a really special recipe for dinner.

HELPS FOR THE COOK

▪ Make a spoon rest from a small colorful sponge; put it on your range when you're cooking and stirring. The sponge is right there to wipe up any spills, and it's easily rinsed out at dishwashing time.

Or make a disposable spoon rest by folding a sheet of paper toweling into a small pad.

▪ When you restock the baby food shelf, date the older jars with a soft pencil to remind you to use them first. This is also a good idea when you restock other canned goods.

▪ Put legs on a large wooden pastry board, and set it on a kitchen table that is too low for working comfort. Metal doorstops make sturdy legs, and they will raise the work surface about four inches.

■ Use one side of your small cutting board to chop fruits and vegetables, the other side for onions and garlic.

■ When frying tiny sausages, fasten four or five in a row with toothpicks, so you can turn several at once. Saves you cooking time, and the small links will brown evenly.

■ Slip your flour sifter into a plastic bag before putting it away in the cupboard.

■ To shave chocolate finely, use a potato peeler—quicker than a knife or grater.

■ Use colorful trays instead of place mats for busy-day family meals. The trays catch any spills and speed up table clearing.

■ Keep waffles crisp and warm when you make them ahead of time by storing them in the oven. Spread baked waffles, unstacked, on a cookie sheet in a warm (250°) oven. None of the family will have to wait for a waffle if you have some made ahead.

■ To grind raw meat easily, cut meat into chunks, wrap loosely in waxed paper and freeze it—but not stone hard. Then grind quickly before frost melts. By the time ground meat is seasoned and molded into loaves or

"What is there to eat? I keep a list of available goodies magnetized to the door of the refrigerator. Whoever eats the last of anything crosses it off the list."

croquettes, meat is unfrozen and ready for cooking. Especially helpful if you are grinding raw liver.

∎ Keep mashed potatoes hot by putting them in a double boiler over hot water; keep pan on very low heat. Potatoes stay hot and fluffy. This helps if your meal has many last-minute details. Also handy if you must hold some potatoes for a latecomer.

∎ Grind frozen cranberries for relish. Juice won't squirt as it does when berries are fresh.

∎ Separate sticky dried fruit by putting it in a warm oven for a few minutes. Dates, figs or raisins will come apart and the wrapping paper can be removed easily.

∎ To distribute seasonings evenly through bread crumbs for stuffing, combine all the seasonings in a large salt shaker and blend. Shake over the crumbs when you mix stuffing.

∎ For deviled eggs, use a wire cheese cutter to slice the hard-cooked eggs in half. The cut is smooth and yolk doesn't crumble.

∎ When you prepare deviled eggs in large quantities, put the yolks through a ricer or food mill. It's faster than mashing them by hand with a fork.

∎ Baked apples and peppers keep their shapes better when baked in greased muffin pans.

- When you grate cheese or vegetables, protect your thumb with a large thimble or a rubber thumb guard (the kind secretaries use).

- Mix French dressing in an 8-ounce baby's nursing bottle. You can measure ingredients easily against the ounce markings on the side of the bottle.

- Quick way to make fine bread crumbs for breading meat and other foods is to break slices of bread, first crisped in oven, into a food mill or potato ricer. A twist of the wrist and the crumbs are ready.

- Turn a colander upside down over frying meat or fish. The small holes allow steam to escape, but grease can't spatter about.

- Poach eggs for the family in a six-cup muffin pan with a non-stick lining. Set the muffin pan with eggs in 1" of water in the electric frypan. Cover frypan to poach the eggs.

- Put popped corn in a deep-fat fryer basket and shake to remove unpopped kernels. Do this when you make popcorn balls or when you serve popcorn to small children.

- Ever change the control setting on your refrigerator—to freeze ice cream or to defrost the unit? Tie a piece of bright ribbon to the door handle. It reminds you to return temperature to normal setting.

■ When cooking dumplings, use a glass oven-ware plate for a cover. You can peek without lifting the lid and making dumplings fall.

■ If you want extra dumplings to serve with soup or stew, you can steam them in an egg poacher. Grease the cups and drop a spoonful of dumpling dough into each. Cover and steam for 10 minutes.

■ Use a roaster pan with cover as a steamer for a large pudding mold. Place mold on rack in roaster. Add a few inches of water, cover and steam on top of the range. Use also for individual pudding molds.

■ If butter is too firm to spread, use your potato peeler to cut thin slices from a stick. Butter slices soften in a jiffy.

■ Keep the kitchen cool by using the electric frypan, rather than the oven, when you cook a small roast or meat loaf or bake a few potatoes. Use frypan for scalloped potatoes, too.

■ Save fingers of worn-out rubber gloves to slip on your thumb for paring vegetables.

■ Put homemade soft drinks in bottles and store them in the refrigerator so children can help themselves. Save used salad dressing bottles and small catsup bottles with caps for this. These hold one serving each and make the drinks more interesting than beverages served in a glass. Have straws handy, too.

- Keep an ice bucket full of ice beside the sink in summer. It saves frequent emptying of ice trays and fuel-consuming opening of the refrigerator. Cubes keep up to 6 or 8 hours in a plastic foam container.

- Use your bun warmer to freshen and soften marshmallows. Place marshmallows in foil-lined basket of warmer. Pour 3 tablespoons of water in the warmer, replace basket and set over low heat, just as you do for buns.

- Keep a food grinder with clamp from marring a counter or table. Cut a 4×6″ piece of rubber or plastic from an old range or sink protector. Insert this between clamp and counter. Keeps grinder from slipping, too.

- You can make a disposable roasting rack by punching holes in the bottom of a foil pie pan. Invert this pan in your Dutch oven.

- Use a mechanic's small oil can (from an auto supply store) for dispensing cooking and salad oil. It squirts small quantities without spilling.

- Teach young cooks to separate eggs by letting them practice with eggs that are to be scrambled. If a bit of yolk gets into the whites, it won't spoil the product.

- Turn meat with tongs or other blunt instrument, rather than a fork. You won't puncture the meat and let the juices escape.

"When you need bits of bacon, cut across the end of the bacon slices. You get many small pieces, and the rest is still in slices."

81

■ If pressed for time when making gelatin dessert, dissolve a package of fruit-flavored gelatin in 1 cup of hot water; then add 1 level cup of chopped ice and water. This hastens setting.

■ Mold gelatin for a potluck supper in cupcake liners or paper cups. The individual servings are easy to handle and keep the gelatin separated from other food on the plate.

NEW TWISTS WITH FOOD

■ Slim pretzel sticks can take the place of toothpicks for serving cubes of cheese or meat as hors d'oeuvres.

■ For a tasty appetizer, dip, whip together in the electric mixer 6 tablespoons of Roquefort or blue cheese dressing and 1 pound of creamed cottage cheese.

■ Wrap any extra poultry stuffing in aluminum foil, add a little water for more moisture and place in the roasting pan with the fowl.

■ When preparing Welsh rabbit, make a double batch and store part in the refrigerator. It's a tasty sauce for broccoli, asparagus or cauliflower, or to serve on toast.

■ For a quick meal of creamed eggs on toast, heat a can of condensed cream of mushroom soup with milk to make it the consistency of medium white sauce. Slice hard-cooked eggs into the soup, heat and serve.

■ Use leftover syrup from a jar of sweet or dill pickles for new flavors. Pour syrup over ham before baking; add it to a sauce for sweet-sour beets; use it to thin mayonnaise for coleslaw. Marinate onion rings in the juice, and chill for 24 hours before serving. You also can use pickle syrup in French dressing; it adds flavor to salads.

■ Make a container for mayonnaise from a large green or sweet red pepper. Cut a thin slice from the stem end, clean out the inside and fill with dressing. This looks attractive on a salad platter.

■ Give toasted cheese sandwiches a new taste. Sprinkle cheese with chopped chives or shredded green pepper, then toast.

■ Add variety to mashed potatoes by stirring in a bouillon cube (chicken or beef) dissolved in the hot milk.

■ Try using drained potato water plus dry milk as the liquid for mashed potatoes.

■ Save leftover mashed potatoes to make cream of potato soup. Add milk gradually to the desired consistency. Season with a lump of butter and onion salt.

■ When a recipe calls for a sharp Cheddar cheese and you have only a mild one, add a bit of pepper, dry mustard and Worcestershire sauce. You'll have a sharp cheese flavor.

■ Make an easy-to-fix fruit salad. Combine ½ cup commercial sour cream; ¼ cup currant jelly, beaten; 1 tablespoon lemon juice; and ⅛ teaspoon salt. Pour dressing over chilled canned fruit (drained) arranged on lettuce.

■ Put pineapple tidbits or shredded coconut in the syrup that's left when all the maraschino cherries are used from a bottle. Let stand a few hours; use as a garnish for fruit cup or fruit salad.

■ Add a grated potato to your meat loaf in place of cracker crumbs. The potato makes a more moist meat loaf.

■ Here's a new way with oyster stew. Put oysters into the blender a few seconds before cooking. You'll have a flavorful stew minus the whole oysters some people dislike.

■ Make and freeze some white sauce cubes for use later. Blend 1 cup softened butter with 1 cup flour. Spread evenly in a refrigerator tray; chill. Cut into 16 cubes and store in the freezer. For thin white sauce, drop a cube into 1 cup hot milk and cook, stirring, until mixture is thick.

"Don't save your paper plates and cups for picnics. Use them for evening meals when you're all in."

■ After coring apples for baking, insert the empty corer in brown sugar and fill it about ¾ full. Replace it in the center of the apple and tap gently. The sugar filling slips neatly into place.

■Use leftover cranberry sauce to fill the holes in apples for baking.

■Want a new flavor sauce to top your steamed puddings? Add ½ cup moist coconut (flaked or shredded, cut into short lengths) to hard sauce. Or dissolve several pieces of butter-rum flavored candy in a hot sauce.

■Peach puffs help perk up a meal. To make, fill peach halves with grated process Cheddar cheese and salad dressing; broil until filling is brown and puffy.

■For a quick family or company dessert, make a chocolate cookie crumb pie shell and fill with peppermint ice cream; drizzle with thick chocolate sauce.

■Add chopped maraschino cherries (about 6) and some maraschino syrup to a rhubarb pie.

■Use some maraschino cherry juice in a tart cherry pie. Juice should be measured as part of the required amount of liquid.

■Make a blue cheese topping for mincemeat or fruit pie. Whip 1 cup heavy cream. Fold in 1 (4-ounce) package blue cheese, crumbled. Freeze. Remove from freezer 10 minutes before serving. Spoon over top of warm pie.

■Add crunchiness to oatmeal cookies by toasting the oatmeal. Spread oatmeal in shallow pan and toast in the oven.

"Add finely grated raw carrots to vegetable soup before serving. They give the soup a rich color and add flavor and texture."

■For crispy nibbles, melt ¼ cup butter or margarine in skillet. Mix in 1 tablespoon dry salad dressing mix (onion or garlic flavor). Remove from heat; stir in 4 cups ready-to-eat, bite-size cereal. Salt to taste.

BAKING SESSIONS

■Place all ingredients to the right of your mixing bowl before you start to measure and mix ingredients for a cake or other recipe. As you use each item, move it to the left of the bowl. Make this a habit, and you'll never have to worry about what you've put in or left out of the cake, even if you are interrupted by the telephone or doorbell.

■Save bowl washing when beating eggs for a cake or cookies. Push creamed shortening and sugar aside; beat eggs in same bowl.

■When mixing cold shortening with an electric mixer, heat mixer blades in hot water for a few minutes. Prevents clogging the blades.

■When baking, break eggs into your measuring cup first, dump them out, and then measure the shortening. The shortening won't stick to the cup, but will slip out easily.

■When a recipe calls for melted shortening, melt it in the pan in which the bread or cake is to be baked. Saves washing an extra utensil and time used in greasing the pan.

▪ You can make a large heart-shaped cake without a special mold. Fill an 8″ square and an 8″ round pan with batter to equal depths. After baking, cut the round cake in half. Place cut edges of the half circles along two adjoining sides of the square cake to form a heart. Frost and decorate the cake with a pastry tube, colored sugar or coconut to emphasize the heart shape.

▪ Remove one oven shelf to use as a cooling rack for baked goods. You can cool extra cakes or pies on inverted muffin pans, too.

▪ Melt chocolate for baking in aluminum foil. Form a cup from foil and butter it lightly. Put chocolate in cup and place in oven, which is turned to preheat. You can slide melted chocolate off foil into mixing bowl, and there's no extra pan to wash.

▪ To cut dates easily, use scissors dipped in hot water. Or, if recipe calls for flour, you can roll the dates in some of the sifted dry ingredients before cutting them. Flour keeps date pieces from sticking to each other or to the cutting edge.

▪ Make your own disposable pastry brush. Fold a piece of paper toweling for the "brush" and clip it in a spring-type clothespin which serves as the brush handle. When the job is finished, toss the soaked piece of toweling away. There's no greasy brush to wash.

■ Bend down the tines of an old long-handled picnic fork to form hooks. Use this to pull hot pans from the back of the oven without burning your arm.

■ Make cake layers more uniform by marking the batter level on the sides of your pans. Scratch a line ½″ from the top of each pan.

■ Use a clean string for slicing pinwheel rolls or jelly rolls off a long, filled roll of pastry. Place center of string under the roll where you want to slice. Bring ends up over the top, cross string, and pull quickly to cut down through the roll. An Ohio woman says it's easier than using a knife.

■ When you bake a loaf or sheet cake, dip out enough batter to make one or two cupcakes (if you have one or two children). The batter isn't missed, and the cupcakes satisfy the children's clamor for a piece of cake right away. A good idea if you're baking for a cake sale. (If you use a muffin pan, put water in the empty sections before baking.)

■ Use your metal measuring cups for baking cupcakes when you have a little more batter than will go into muffin pans. The ⅓-cup and ½-cup sizes work nicely.

Or try paper baking cups, set in rims of self-sealing jar lids and placed on a cookie sheet. Rims of a matching size will keep batter-filled paper cups from spreading.

■Make a batch of fortune cupcakes for a party. Write the fortunes on small strips of paper and roll tightly in pieces of waxed paper. Insert one in the center of each cupcake before you frost it.

■Make alphabet cake blocks for your child's birthday party. Frost a loaf cake, and cut it in squares. With a different colored frosting, print a letter on each block to spell the child's name and "Happy Birthday." Arrange the blocks on a tray for a centerpiece. Insert each birthday candle in a separate block.

■When you frost a cake, use metal skewers instead of toothpicks to hold layers in place. After frosting is set, skewers can be removed. There's no danger of someone biting into a forgotten toothpick.

■Frost cupcakes the easy way by dipping top of cupcake into the frosting. Give it a good quick twirl.

■Brush angel food cake lightly with a small pastry brush to remove loose crumbs before icing. Frost first with a thin coat of icing, let dry, and frost again. You'll have a smooth, crumbless finish.

■When you frost cookies or cupcakes with different colored frostings, use the sections of a muffin pan or a child's feeding dish to separate the various colors.

"To save time when baking, I bought an extra set of beaters for my electric mixer. I don't have to stop and wash beaters after cake batter is mixed and I'm ready to whip egg whites or frosting."

- When making large cookies, such as gingerbread men or animal shapes, roll dough directly on the cookie sheet. After cutting out shapes, simply remove the scraps. If the cookie sheet has a raised edge, turn it over and use the reverse side for rolling and baking.

- Last-rolled cookies often are tough because of extra flour they absorb in handling. Avoid this by using confectioner's sugar instead of flour on board and rolling pin.

- Cut cookie dough into squares or diamond shapes with a pastry wheel. The cookies have nice fluted edges and there are no scraps for you to reroll.

- Bake holiday cookies to be hung on the Christmas tree with a dried bean in the hole of the cookie. The bean keeps the hole open as the cookie bakes.

- Here's a cookie baking tip if you have small children in the family. Make the first pan of cookies smaller than usual and without nuts. You can add nuts to the remaining dough if you like.

- Save broken bits of cookies and crumbs in a plastic bag stored in the refrigerator. Before long, there's enough to make a piecrust. Roll crumbs fine and follow directions for a graham cracker crust. You can combine different cookies, such as gingersnaps and vanilla wafers.

This combination is good with vanilla cream filling.

▪ Crush cookies or crackers for crumbs in a plastic bag. You can easily see how fine the crumbs are, and the rolling pin stays clean. Of course, the blender is great for making crumbs—fast.

▪ Firm a crumb crust in a pie plate by pressing a slightly smaller pie plate against it. Rotate the smaller plate lightly before removing, so it will come up clean.

▪ Easy way to handle piecrust is to roll it on waxed paper. Instead of turning the dough, turn the whole paper. Use the paper also to transfer crust to pan.

▪ To prevent a single crust from buckling, first prick unbaked pastry with a fork. Then cross two strips of aluminum foil on top of pastry to extend over edge of pie plate. Place a smaller pie plate on top. When crust begins to brown, lift foil strips to remove the top plate.

▪ Put custard pie filling into a pitcher or large glass measuring cup. Pour into the crust after crust is placed in the oven. Much easier than carrying a filled pie plate.

▪ Pumpkin pies cook quickly and evenly when the pumpkin mixture is heated before it is poured into the pie shell.

▪To prevent sogginess in fruit or custard pies, brush the bottom crust with unbeaten egg white. The same coating will add a glaze to the top crust of a pie.

▪Bubbling juice from a berry pie won't overflow during baking if you cut paper drinking straws in thirds and insert them in the slits in the top crust. Or use macaroni in the slits.

▪A narrow strip of foil folded over the edge of a piecrust keeps it from becoming too brown before the pie filling is done.

▪Avoid a "weepy" meringue when you're making a cream pie and don't have time to let the filling cool. Place bowl of egg whites in a pan of hot water while you beat. The meringue will then be warm enough to prevent condensation (weeping) when you spread it on the filling.

▪When cutting a meringue pie, use a knife that has been lightly coated with butter or brushed with oil on both sides of the blade. There will be no sticking or tearing to spoil the appearance of the meringue.

▪Before wrapping a meringue pie or a cake that has soft frosting, stick toothpicks into the top. Leave enough height so paper rests on toothpicks and not on the topping.

▪Make apple dumplings with scraps of left-over pastry. Pare and core an apple; place it

"Since my family likes the flavor and color of unpeeled apples, I simply wash, core and slice apples that go into pies."

on rolled-out pastry; fill apple with sugar, spice, raisins and a dot of butter. Seal pastry at top, wrap in foil and freeze. Bake when you have enough to serve the family.

▪ Spread leftover piecrust with peanut butter and roll it like a jelly roll. Cut into ¼″ slices; bake in 400° oven. It's a special snack treat for the children—or you.

▪ Cover a cream pie lightly with waxed paper while the filling cools. Prevents a crust from forming on top.

▪ Put greased bread dough to rise in a large plastic bag. Dough won't stick to the bag, and it stays moist so no crust will form.

▪ Store dough for refrigerator rolls in a three-pound shortening can. The can takes up less space than a bowl and its tight cover prevents a crust from forming.

▪ Fancy sweet rolls can be made by rolling out dough and cutting shapes with cookie cutters. Most children love the variety.

▪ Cut "figure eight" yeast rolls with a dough-nut cutter. Pick up the ring, stretch it, then twist. No ends to tuck under.

▪ When cutting out raised doughnuts, drop three centers into each buttered section of a muffin pan. You can have cloverleaf rolls as well as the doughnuts.

"Add crushed pineapple to the next apple pie you make. Spread 4 or more tablespoons of the pineapple over the sliced apples. Then put on the top crust."

■ Cut biscuit dough in squares with a sharp knife instead of using a round cutter. It's quicker, biscuits are attractive, and there are no trimmings to remold and cut—a step that results in second-class biscuits.

■ To make shortcake in your electric waffle baker, use drop-biscuit batter. Saves heating the oven and gives rich, crisp shortcake.

YOUR FREEZER AT WORK

■ When you have lemons and oranges that might spoil, squeeze and freeze the juice in ice cube trays. Later, you can thaw as many cubes as you need.

■ If you have trouble crumbling blue or Roquefort cheese, freeze cheese—2 hours to overnight—then grate. Freeze only the amount you will need for a recipe.

■ To be sure of having buttermilk on hand for favorite recipes, a Missouri homemaker measures the milk in ⅓-cup and ½-cup portions and freezes it. She removes frozen portions from containers, wraps, labels and stores them until needed.

■ Freeze unused pimientos from an opened jar or can. Break off frozen pieces when you want to add a touch of color to a casserole. Pimientos will spoil after a time in the refrigerator, even when covered with oil.

▪ You can freeze unsweetened fruit juice in ice cube trays, then add the cubes to lemonade for extra color and flavor.

▪ Use small quantities of fresh fruit (one kind or a combination) for frozen ice-cream toppings. To make raspberry, strawberry or blackberry topping, wash fruit and crush until the juice begins to run. Add sugar to taste and mix thoroughly. Pack, label and freeze. To serve, spoon over ice cream before topping is completely thawed.

▪ If ice cream is soft when you get home from the store, dip out servings on a cookie sheet with an ice-cream scoop and freeze the servings. When the ice-cream balls are firm, put them in a covered container and return them to the freezer. Ice cream is in individual portions, ready for serving.

▪ Pack refrigerator cookie dough in small, well-greased soup cans; store in freezer until ready to bake. Then cut out bottom of can; push out dough and slice it. You'll have perfectly round cookies.

▪ A California homemaker says she is left with enough cooked food after each dinner to feed one person. She puts it in a foil pan, covers it with aluminum foil and freezes it. In several days she has frozen enough homemade TV dinners to serve the family on an extremely hectic day.

■When you prepare stuffing, double the recipe. Freeze the extra in one-cup portions; use it to stuff chops, fish, rolled steak.

■Leftover egg whites can be frozen in foil-lined muffin cups. When set, remove filled foil cups, fold tops to close, pack in a round carton and return to freezer.

■Mold hamburger patties on a cookie sheet, then freeze. Remove patties from the cookie sheet and pack in a plastic bag, tightly secured with a rubber band or wire twist. Return to freezer. Take out one—or a dozen—as you need meat for a meal.

■When packaging meat for the freezer, slip each hand into a plastic bag for handling the meat. You won't have to wash your hands before you seal and label a package.

■Before you stack packages of one kind of food in your freezer, number them consecutively with No. 1 at the bottom. Then you'll know, as you remove them, how many packages of that food are left in the freezer.

■When freezing a quantity of broiler-fryer chickens, cut them into serving pieces, wrap each piece individually in plastic wrap and quick-freeze. Then put all wings in one large plastic bag, all legs in another and so on. Label and date each bag. You can make a quick selection of pieces when you need them.

"When you bake for the freezer, make a white or yellow cake first, then use the same bowl and beaters—without washing—for a chocolate cake."

■ Cut up a stewing hen and put pieces in a large roaster pan. Add salt and pepper and twigs of sage, rosemary and marjoram. Cover pan and cook in a slow oven until tender. Remove meat from bones (save bones for broth). Pack meat in containers for the freezer—in amounts needed for casseroles and salads.

■ Make ice cream that has few ice crystals by first partially freezing the milk in an ice cube tray. Then pour milk into a chilled bowl, add other ingredients and beat with mixer on high speed until creamy. Put mixture in ice cube tray to freeze. It need only be stirred once during freezing to make it smooth and creamy.

■ When you make pies for freezing, cut initials in the top crusts—A for apple, B for blueberry, C for cherry, etc. Then wrap pies in plastic wrap so initials can be seen at a glance.

■ For compact cookie storage in the freezer, pack the cookies in a row in cartons left from waxed paper or aluminum foil.

■ Ready-to-bake drop cookies keep in your freezer. Make up your favorite recipe and drop batter on cookie sheet. (You can place cookies close together for this.) Freeze the unbaked cookies, then transfer them to plastic bags for freezer storage. You can have fresh-baked cookies in a few minutes.

"The freezer makes it absolutely necessary that you spend that extra few minutes in bed. You must decide what to thaw, and early in the day."

■Change the flavor of vanilla ice cream by blending 1 cup mincemeat with a half gallon of softened vanilla ice cream. Freeze. Serve topped with warm caramel sauce.

■Freeze fresh fruits in season to be used later in jams and jellies. Measure number of cups of crushed or cut-up fruit or juice your recipe requires, pour into bread pans and freeze without sugar. (A water pack is suggested for peaches. Slice peaches, pack in containers, cover with cold water containing 1 teaspoon ascorbic acid per quart of water.) Remove frozen blocks of fruit or juice from pans; wrap, label and store in the freezer. Blocks stack well. When ready to make jelly or jam, melt blocks of fruit or juice and proceed with your recipe.

■Slice cake or nut and fruit breads before freezing. Put plastic wrap between the slices. It's easy to remove the number of slices you need, and they thaw quickly.

■When freezing vegetables in the summer, fill some containers with layers of different vegetables to use for soup or succotash.

■Your electric French fryer is fine for blanching vegetables before freezing. Heat water in fryer to boiling. Immerse fryer basket filled with vegetables.

Or use your lettuce basket for blanching and cooling vegetables. Handle with tongs.

■ Fill tall aluminum water tumblers with water, then freeze. Unmold these "logs" of ice to use for cooling blanched vegetables. Or put them an an insulated jug to keep a beverage cool all day at a picnic.

■ Quick-freeze corn, peas or blueberries in a shallow tray. Store the frozen food in plastic freezer bags. The small pieces are loose; you can dip out the amount you need.

■ Label foods for freezing with a "use before" date. You can tell which to use first; foods won't be too long in the freezer.

■ Keep contents moving in and out of the freezer for best use of space. Use bulky cuts of meat containing bones ahead of boneless cuts which take up less room. Freeze soups in concentrated form; dilute to taste when ready to serve.

■ A variety of colored rubber bands can help you identify many items in your freezer. Use red bands to fasten plastic bags covering cherry pies, blue bands for blueberry pies, and yellow for peach pies. Also use rubber bands of a single color to fasten bags of each batch of bread or rolls. You can tell which bread is older and should be used first.

■ Choose different colored cords to help you identify meat in your freezer. Wrap beef with red cord, pork with white, etc.

■List contents of your upright freezer on a chart that shows the shelf arrangement. Tape chart to the door so you can check locations before you open the door.

■Draw a map showing location of your chest freezer contents, as a Pennsylvania woman does. She stacks similar items from the bottom up. Extra pies, cakes and bread are spread over the top, so the map helps her find what she wants without shifting everything in the top layer.

■A Minnesota woman keeps track of freezer contents with a pegboard. She has hooks inserted at 3″ intervals; under each hook is the name of a frozen food. On the hook she hangs as many metal washers as she has packages of that item. Her pegboard is over the freezer. When food is removed, she takes off a corresponding washer.

Or keep a blackboard inventory—with chalk and eraser to change the numbers as you remove or add items.

■To thaw frozen meat quickly, put it in a plastic bag; close bag tightly and set it in warm water. This is especially helpful in separating frozen chops or thawing ground meat to make patties.

■Keep heavy cotton work gloves to protect your hands while you are rearranging food in the freezer.

"Make a quantity of spaghetti sauce and freeze most of it. You can use it in spaghetti, lasagna, macaroni-and-cheese casserole, hamburger pie—and many other things you'll think of."

■ Use your automatic electric toaster to thaw frozen bread slices quickly. Set toaster control at "light." Bread slices will come out thawed, but not toasted.

■ If you have to defrost your freezer, wear an old pair of fabric gloves under rubber gloves. Hands stay warm and dry.

■ An electric roaster is well insulated and can be used for storing frozen food while a freezer is defrosting. Close all vents in the roaster, place trays of ice on the bottom, then pack food on top of the ice.

CAN IT

■ Put whole spices in a large aluminum tea infuser instead of a cheesecloth bag when making pickles or catsup. It's easy to remove spices and to clean the holder.

■ An oven baster can be used to take excess liquid out of jars when you are canning. Helps keep top of jars clean.

■ If you can foods in quantity, make a list of the foods and number of jars. Tape the list to the inside of a cupboard door—handy, so you can cross off items as you use each jar. You'll always know how many you have left. If you run out of an item during the winter, list it at the bottom under heading: "More needed next year."

"During canning season, I put up fruit juices and pulp. When the weather is cooler and I have more time, I make these into butters and jellies."

101

■ When you make sauerkraut, use a double plastic bag (one bag inside another) as a cover. Fill inner bag with water and fasten securely with a string. The bags should be of heavyweight, watertight plastic used for freezing foods. They should be large enough to cover the cabbage and fit tightly against the sides of the container. The bag-cover keeps air from the surface of the kraut, prevents growth of yeasts and molds, and keeps cabbage submerged in the brine.

■ For straining fruit juice for jelly, use a nylon laundry bag of fine mesh (the kind sold for washing hose and lingerie) instead of cheesecloth. The bag can be reused.

■ Slip plastic bags on your hands when you squeeze fruit juice for jelly. The juice won't stain your hands, and you can handle the mixture while it's still quite hot.

■ As you seal jelly, place a clean thread or string loosely across the jar before you add the paraffin. When you want to serve the jelly, just pull the string to loosen seal and lift the paraffin.

■ Line a pan with foil when you use it to melt paraffin. After unused wax hardens, fold foil around it and store for future use. (Never place pan of paraffin directly on heat—paraffin is too flammable. Put the pan over water; a double boiler is best.)

PICNIC MEALS

■ Use a muffin pan to hold the fixings, such as mustard, catsup, relish, chopped onions, mayonnaise and pickles when you eat outdoors. You won't have to pass a lot of separate bottles and jars.

■ To keep sweet corn piping hot for picnics at home, put a turkey-size plastic bag on a large serving platter. Using tongs, stack the hot corn pyramid-style inside the bag. Fasten the bag with a spring-type clothespin. The corn stays hot until the last delicious ear has been served.

■ A Michigan family takes individual lunches on family picnics. Each person is responsible for his own lunch box and thermos and can take his favorite beverage, sandwiches, fruit and cookies. It's easier for Mom than having to prepare all the food by herself.

■ Stack several dishes of food in a picnic basket by using a wire cooling rack between layers. Rack rests on top edge of one dish and supports the dish above.

■ When taking a covered dish to a picnic or church supper, set the container in the center of a large sturdy dish towel, bring up the opposite corners and tie in a tight knot. No danger of burns or spills and the knot makes a handy handle.

■ Making lemonade for a picnic? Mix part of it ahead of time and pour into ice cube trays to freeze. Use the frozen lemonade to ice the rest so the drink won't get weak and watery as the cubes melt.

■ Pack a sharp knife safely for carrying. Make a holder from two strips of cardboard, the width of the blade, and seal edges together with masking tape.

■ Fill clean 1-gallon plastic bleach jugs about ¾ full of water and place in the freezer. Use ice-filled jugs in portable refrigerator in place of block ice. Water in the jugs from melted ice can be used for rinsing picnic dishes and utensils.

■ Your plastic dishpan will serve as a large picnic salad bowl or a carryall for silver and napkins. Or it's useful for carrying ice and bottled drinks.

■ Fasten wheels to your picnic table legs at one end of the table. You can pick up the other end and move it easily. Wheels from an old tricycle or baby buggy will do.

■ A Florida family has a picnic tablecloth made of unbleached muslin. On it they have labeled appropriate spots with a laundry marker: "Where's the salt and pepper?"— "How about the butter?"—"Cream and sugar go here!" At one end, they added "Salad bar—

help yourself." For odd things, they wrote, "Ask for it; maybe we've got it." The cloth reminds the family to collect all necessary items before the meal begins.

For a large crowd, you can use this idea to mix the group. On a long cloth, write "His," "Hers," "His," etc.

■ Use a colorful bed sheet as a washable tablecloth for a picnic or party.

■ Run a drawstring through the hem of your picnic tablecloth to keep it in place. Or fit it like a contour sheet so it slips on and off the table easily, yet won't blow off.

■ Keep four spring-type clothespins as part of your picnic gear. After you cover the picnic table with a cloth, fold the cloth under each corner and fasten it securely with a clothespin.

"Spur-of-the-minute picnics with sandwiches made right at the picnic, usually turn out more fun than a planned excursion. A meal of fried chicken, homemade salad and other goodies prepared ahead of time may also include a tired, cross mother."

*"No-iron clothes aren't really a
new idea. I remember when my
children were little, I sometimes
folded the wash and sat on it."*

Laundry Time

Laundry Time

*Those Blue Mondays may be gone,
but you still have clothes to wash*

Nobody wants to go back to the "good old days" when it comes to clothing and laundry equipment. Easy-care fabrics and easy-to-run washers and dryers take the chore out of keeping everyone in clean clothes. In fact, you're probably washing more clothes, towels and rugs each week than your great-grandmothers ever did—because you can. Everyone in the family wants clean underwear and socks every day, and you run the curtains through a cycle whenever they look dusty.

Laundry still isn't done by magic—in spite of all the "miracle" fibers that surround us. You do have to measure the right amount of detergent and set the machines to do the job. You have to know washing procedures and about treating stains, if everything is to stay looking its best.

WASH AND DRY

▪ For playclothes and other things that are very dirty, use a 30-minute soak period with warm water and detergent. Agitate the load a few minutes at the beginning. Later, drain the sudsy water and wash as usual.

▪ When someone in the family is ill, use a disinfectant in the wash water. For most washable fabrics, liquid chlorine bleach will do the job; follow directions on the label. Check label also for fabrics, such as wool and silk, that aren't safe in this bleach.

■ Try plastic wastebaskets in bedrooms to serve as individual laundry hampers. Or use string shopping bags that can hang from hooks, door knobs or clothes hangers.

You can fashion a laundry hamper from a shopping bag, too. Put two hangers on a closet rod; loop the bag handles over them.

■ In your laundry area, have several large baskets, bins or hampers to help sort the wash as it collects. If you can have four baskets, for instance, use one for white things, one for colored fabrics and a third for extra-dirty clothes. Save the fourth basket to hold clean things to be ironed.

■ Keep a small box in your laundry room for collecting pencils, combs, paper clips and other items that turn up in the pockets of clothing headed for the washer. Owners know where to claim things.

■ Turn dresses inside out before you put them in the washer. This avoids any tangling of ties, belts and sashes.

■ Before washing stained clothing, baste around the stain with colored thread. When fabric is wet, you will be able to find the stain to give it special attention.

■ If you have boys in the family, keep T-shirts separated by sewing a different color thread in the neck of each size.

"During a recent illness I discovered that absolutely nothing adverse happens if the sheets don't get changed for two weeks."

109

■ Wash white things together in a separate load, if you can. Colored fabrics often bleed a bit, even though you can't detect it in the water. White things, especially synthetic fabrics, pick up the stray dye.

■ When washing slipcovers, rub shampoo (hair or upholstery) into spots on the back and arms where oily heads and hands have rested. Let this stand for about 20 minutes, then wash as usual. This shampoo treatment removes oil spots that the regular laundry procedure often won't get out.

■ Before laundering curtains with pin-type hooks, indicate places where pins go with a laundry marker or with thread. This saves time when you replace the pins.

■ When you launder café curtains, run a heavy cord through the washable rings on each section and tie them together. This prevents rings from pulling out in the washer.

■ You can shampoo your best scatter rugs outdoors on the picnic table. Rugs dry flat, with no clothesline creases.

■ Wash a plastic shower curtain or liner in warm sudsy water. Do it in the bathtub or in an automatic washer (for about 3 minutes). If you use the machine, let it spin a little—just long enough to drain out the sudsy water. Then give the curtain a rinse.

■ Tie or button wet sneakers or canvas play shoes together and hang them over a line to dry. They will dry faster, and the soles will not have time to mildew.

■ Dry small rugs or blankets on the line without creases. Save tubes from paper towels, foil wrap or waxed paper. Slit the rolls down the side and slip over line.

■ A multiple skirt hanger is handy for drying wet mittens—ones you've just washed or ones that come in from play.

■ Before putting clothing with heavy buckles and buttons into the dryer, turn the clothes inside out; secure with safety pins. This prevents the metal from damaging the dryer drum.

■ To dry a woolen sweater, first squeeze out excess moisture by rolling sweater in a turkish towel. Then place the sweater flat on a plastic tablecloth. A New York woman spreads a tablecloth over her bed and dries several sweaters on it at once.

■ Hang slacks by legs to dry. Garment weight removes wrinkles, means less pressing.

■ Develop a laundry pick-up system to save you steps. In your utility room, designate an individual shelf or colorful plastic dishpan for each child in the family. Stack his clean clothes there; he'll know at a glance when there are things to put away.

THOSE STAINS

▪ Keep an embroidery hoop in the laundry room to hold fabrics taut when you need to remove spots or stains.

▪ To treat most stains, first sponge with cool water. Then work concentrated detergent into the spot. Wash as usual.

▪ When her young son blew an extra-super gum bubble that burst over the front of his shirt, an Illinois mother put the shirt in the freezer. Next morning, she peeled off the brittle gum. (You can use an ice cube to harden the gum for peeling, too.)

▪ If candle wax drips on your tablecloth, let it harden, then scrape off as much as possible. Stretch cloth over a pan and pour boiling water through the spot; hold the teakettle about a foot above the cloth.

▪ Chocolate stains are a familiar sight to most mothers. Sponge the spot with cool water right away. Then work liquid detergent into the area and wash as usual. Use a bleach suited to the fabric if some stain remains.

▪ Removing fruit stains from linen tablecloths usually can be accomplished with boiling water. Hold the cloth taut over a bowl or sink, and pour boiling water from a height of about a foot onto the stain. Keep pouring boiling water until the stain disappears; then wash the cloth as usual. You can use this same method for wine stains.

▪ Take care of coffee spills by sponging the spot with cool water immediately—so the color won't set. Later, you can work in detergent and wash the fabric.

▪ For mildew spots, wash the fabric. Mold growth will weaken fibers, so try to treat the spot while it's still fresh. Dry fabric in the sun, if possible. A bleach treatment may be needed if some stain remains.

▪ Ball-point pen marks usually are in dots or streaks. Avoid rubbing which would cause the stain to spread. Work from the wrong side of the fabric. Make a pad of paper toweling and hold it against the right side of the ink stain. Put liquid detergent on a cloth and push this against the stain from the inside. Keep moving the pad of paper to a clean spot as ink is transferred to it.

▪ Avoid ironing an area that you have treated for stain until after the garment has been washed or cleaned to remove all detergent or other cleaning solutions.

▪ Greasy soil lines on shirt collars, especially those on permanent press fabrics, come out better if you first rub in some liquid detergent or shampoo—or a paste made from a dry laundry detergent and water.

■ For grease stains on permanent press table-cloths, rub liquid detergent into the spot and let it stand for several hours—or overnight. Wash as usual. Repeat this detergent-soak if necessary.

■ Dry-cleaning solvent helps remove grease, even when a fabric is washable. Apply solvent to treat spot first, then launder the garment.

EASIER IRONING

■ As you sprinkle laundry to be ironed, put clothing for each family member in a separate plastic bag. This is a time-saver when some-one needs an item in a hurry.

■ As you iron tablecloths, fold them in thirds so there is a flat section in the middle. If you omit a fold in the center, table decorations can rest on a level area.

■ Use a plastic cloth, about 54″ square, under your ironing table when you do tablecloths and other large pieces. Or place a card table under the small end of your ironing table to keep these large pieces off the floor.

■ When ironing curtain panels or tablecloths, turn the ironing table so you work on the wide part. Rest iron on narrow end.

■ To give sheets an ironed look, press just the border on the top one.

114

■ If you want to touch up fitted sheets, place all four corners together, one inside the other. They'll form a peak that fits over the small end of the ironing table, making them easier to iron and fold.

■ Use a tray table to hold finished flat work. Later, pick up the table with the ironed things and carry it to drawers and shelves.

If you have a kitchen utility cart, use that for stacking and delivering the ironing.

■ To fit an ironing table cover snugly, lace a cord through sturdy safety pins attached to the cover on the underside of the table. Line up the pins opposite each other. It's easy to slip out laces and remove the pins when replacing cover.

■ An adjustable ironing table eliminates backaches you get from bending over one that is too low. You should be able to stand erect.

■ Place a large iron-on patch on the cover where you rest the iron. Patch should last as long as the cover.

■ Use both hands when you iron. By shifting the iron to your left hand, you can reach all parts of the table, even when seated.

■ Two strips of elastic, on the underside of your ironing table, make a holder for your press cloth. Attach the elastic to the table frame or pin it to the cover.

■A small hook holds a lint brush at the end of your ironing table.

■You'll find distilled water for your steam iron in the dehumidifier. (Be sure to strain water through cheesecloth; this will remove any dust or dirt.)

■Try spray starch for touch-up pressing on cottons between wearings. It's fine for smoothing wrinkled belts, too.

■If your husband likes his shirts starched a little—but not much—use spray starch for the collars, cuffs and fronts.

■When you're faced with a big ironing, especially in warm weather, dampen just enough to do in an hour. You'll be surprised how fast the hour goes and how much you get done. This system decreases the feeling of drudgery you get when you're confronted with a mountain of ironing, some of which you leave unfinished.

■Use a pressing mitt to iron out creases in draperies after they've been hung. Slip mitt on one hand and hold it back of area to be pressed; iron with the other hand.

■Before you press dark clothing, tumble garments in your dryer for a short time. This removes lint and saves brushing time.

■ Use the sticky side of masking tape to remove lint when you press dark clothing.

■ When ironing a man's shirt, button the sleeves together. This keeps them from dragging on the floor as you work.

■ Press neckties without getting them out of shape. Cut a piece of cardboard the shape of the tie and slip it inside. Use a press cloth.

■ A strip of foam rubber comes in handy when ironing. Slip it under pants cuffs and the fly as you iron on the wrong side. You won't press ridges in the fabric.

■ Slip a clean handkerchief into shirt and dress pockets on ironing day. Dad and the children will always have one when they put on clean clothes.

■ Protect your ironing table cover from soil when it's not in use. You can buy a plastic cover—or you can make one. Cut a piece of plastic several inches larger than the ironing surface. Hem it, then run elastic through the hem so it will fit snugly.

■ Make a padded slipcover from old towels for your wooden chopping board. Handy for ironing small items in an emergency.

"I hide my ironing in an armchair in the bedroom so I won't have to look at it. I iron what is needed—more if I have time. I probably will get to the bottom of the chair when the last child finishes college."

"I enjoy sewing. But I like to let my husband think I sew because I'm trying to be smart and thrifty. He doesn't need to know I get such a kick out of it."

Sewing & Mending

Sewing & Mending

Needle, thread and patches help hold the family together

Women have been stitching things by hand and machine for decades. It's a hobby, pastime, status symbol, necessity or chore—depending on your viewpoint. Making your own clothes and furnishings for the house is a popular activity these days. You get exactly what you want (well, almost—depending on what you can find in fabrics and how well you sew). You save money, and you have an original. With the scraps, you can stitch up something for the children.

On the other hand, if sewing isn't your strong point, and if it makes you bite your nails or scream at the kids, maybe you'd better stick to mending and patching. Just enough sewing to hold things together.

In either case, no home should be without some sewing supplies. Even the non-sewer could use a good pincushion, for instance. You even can make one by covering a sponge with some denim or other firm fabric. Pins and needles won't work down inside and get lost as they do in some pincushions.

EQUIPMENT—BIG AND LITTLE

▪ A pincushion in the end of a spool of thread is handy. Push a strip of sponge rubber into one end of the spool, and keep a needle ready for use.

- Sew a strip of elastic to a small pincushion so you can wear it on your wrist. Use it to hold pins as you lay out patterns, assemble pieces for stitching or hang hems.

- A household file with separate compartments for papers provides organized storage for flat sewing notions such as mending tape, elastic, zippers and seam binding.

- Tray tables are useful when you sew. Place one on each side of the sewing machine. Stack cut-out pieces on one table. After you stitch pieces together, move them to the other table.

- A dresser drawer makes a good sewing box. Divide part of it into small compartments for holding thread, needles, zippers, tapes and scissors; leave a large section for storage of your present project. The drawer can be carried to any location where you want to sew. When you're through, return materials to the drawer and replace in the dresser—out of the way.

- Attach a section of tape measure to the front of your sewing machine cabinet in an inconspicuous spot. You can quickly check a zipper length or hem depth.

- If you have a sewing machine without drawers, a new metal fishing-tackle box will hold neatly all necessary supplies. These boxes have a handle, and the upper compartment tray lifts up when the lid is opened.

"Whenever I sew for one of the children, that person takes over kitchen clean-up chores. (This usually turns out to be a two-man operation. The volunteer then is assured of help when I'm sewing for him.)"

■ If your sewing machine is in the family room and you often leave your work in progress, find a way to shield the clutter. You might use a folding screen, painted or papered, to blend with the room.

■ Add a spice cabinet with drawers to your sewing equipment. The small drawers are a good size for loose snaps, hooks and eyes, tailor's chalk and buttons.

■ Keep bobbins under control. For the metal ones, attach a magnetic knife holder to the inside of your sewing machine cabinet door.

For any round bobbins, use a plastic pill bottle (1″ diameter). Stack bobbins inside; you can see all the different colors. You can also string round bobbins on a pipe cleaner or put them on a thin bolt (3″ length is fine). Fasten a nut to the bolt so bobbins will stay in place.

■ Magnets can help hold sewing supplies in place. Put a small magnet in your sewing basket to collect stray straight pins and needles. Use a magnetic knife rack on or near your sewing machine to hold scissors, crochet hooks and metal measuring tools.

■ Attach a rubber suction cup or a piece of foam rubber to the foot pedal of a portable sewing machine. This prevents the pedal from creeping around on a smooth-surface floor when you stitch.

▪Keep a sewing scrapbook with a large piece of fabric and an extra button from every dress you sew for the children. Makes it easy when a patch or button is needed, and your girls will love to look them over.

▪Save baby food jars to hold lace, ribbons, rickrack, etc., in sewing machine drawers.

▪Slippery materials won't slide as you stitch if you secure a turkish towel to your machine table. Fabric will rest on it and stay in place.

▪Keep a spring-type clothespin on your sewing table. Use it to hold pattern pieces together until you are finished with them.

▪When you start a new spool of thread, mark the slit in the spool end with a ball-point pen or a dot of nail polish. You'll always be able to find the spot for fastening the thread. Keeps sewing box neat.

▪Renew a limp tape measure by placing the tape between sheets of waxed paper and pressing it with a warm iron.

▪Clean lint and fuzz from the moving parts of your sewing machine before you oil it. You can use a pastry brush, a typewriter cleaning brush—or a pipe cleaner.

▪After you oil a sewing machine, stitch through a blotter or scraps of fabric several times—in case there is some excess oil.

- Fasten a paper bag to the side of your sewing machine table with a piece of masking tape. Threads and scraps can be brushed into it, and there is no picking up afterward.

- Keep sewing scraps in individual plastic bags. They're easy to identify and don't tangle.

- A Pennsylvania woman saves long stringlike scraps when she cuts out wool garments. These pieces are easily raveled whenever she needs mending thread of matching color.

- Make a sleeveboard for ironing by wrapping a heavy towel around a rolling pin. Fasten towel securely with pins.

- Use a stiff, dampened toothbrush to open newly sewn seams and to flatten lace and rickrack as you iron.

- Tweezers in the sewing box help remove tailor's tacks and hard-to-get threads.

- Corral loose snaps in your sewing box by snapping the parts together over a strip of cheesecloth or paper.

- When buying buttons for a dress you are making, take along a scrap of the fabric with a slit cut in it. If the button is mounted on a card, you can put the slit over the button to check the effect.

- Store one-of-a-kind buttons together on a pipe cleaner.

"My husband taught me to patch his work clothes with fabric glue. What a time-saver."

■ String matching buttons on a thread and tie the ends together before you put them away. Saves hunting for the set later.

■ Keep the tail from a rattail comb with your sewing supplies. Use it for poking out corners in collars and belts after you've stitched and turned them.

SEWING HOW-TO'S

■ When the right and wrong side of a fabric look much the same, chalk an X on the wrong side of all pieces as they are cut. Or apply a small piece of masking (or freezer) tape to the wrong side as you cut each pattern piece. This speeds assembly and assures you having the right side out as you sew.

■ Before cutting fabric with a napped surface such as velvet or corduroy, mark the wrong side with chalk arrows to indicate the way the nap runs. This eliminates the danger of cutting pieces the wrong way.

■ Pin sheer fabric to paper before cutting bias strips. Mark the paper for desired widths of bias, then cut through both the paper and the fabric.

■ To match plaids or stripes for stitching, first iron one seam allowance under. Then lay it along the other seam line, just as it should be matched. Apply transparent tape along the seam line to hold pieces in place. Turn to inside and stitch along the creased line. Peel off the tape before pressing the seam open. This works well for woven fabrics since transparent tape won't stretch.

■ To thread the sewing machine needle, put a piece of white paper under the foot. The eye will show more plainly.

■ Keep a small magnifying glass near your machine to use at needle-threading time.

■ Always thread two bobbins before you start on a large sewing project. You won't have to stop halfway through the job to fill one.

■ Make garment buttons removable by converting them into studs. Sew a small button to the back of each garment button, leaving a short loop between the two (unless garment button has a shank). Work a small buttonhole (to fit the small button) on the underlap of the garment where the button would be sewn.

■ That bottom button on a front-opening dress or skirt is the one that often tears loose as you walk or sit in the garment. Avoid this by first sewing the bottom button to the center of a piece of elastic, about 1″ long. Then, sew the elastic to the dress, with the button in its proper position. This gives enough stretch to prevent tearing; elastic doesn't show when the dress is buttoned.

■ Sew buttons in place with elastic thread (the kind used for shirring). Keeps buttons from tearing out when they are strained.

■ Use elastic thread, double, to make loop buttonholes. Cover with regular thread that matches garment, using the buttonhole stitch. The "give" in the loop makes it easy to slip loops over little round buttons.

■ You can make loop buttonholes from round shoelaces. The laces are inexpensive, wear well and come in several different colors.

■ When making buttonholes by hand, put in a row of machine stitches to give a firm base. Begin stitching slightly off center (about 1 stitch away) from where buttonhole will be cut. Stitch parallel to the buttonhole, turn the corner, take 2 stitches, turn again and continue twice around the rectangle. Tie thread ends; finish buttonhole by hand. Especially good for heavy fabrics.

■ For hand-worked buttonholes, mark the place for each opening with a thin coat of colorless nail polish. When polish is dry, cut through the center and you have straight, non-raveling edges for stitching.

■ If your dress fabric has a mixture of colors, use strands of the predominating hues for making buttonholes. This will blend better than strands of a single color.

■ When you make bound buttonholes with fabric strips, brush a bit of clear fingernail polish on the little triangles at each end before you turn the strips to the wrong side. This prevents raveling at the corners.

■ To lengthen a belt that has become too short, remove the buckle. Add an inch or two of elastic and attach the buckle to it. You have extra length, and the elastic is hidden when you fasten the belt.

■ Metal zippers that stick will often work smoothly if rubbed with wax.

■ To make gathers in a heavy fabric, use heavy-duty thread on the bobbin. Loosen machine tension slightly. Put in two rows of long stitches, then pull up both rows of bobbin threads at once.

■ If organdy slides through the ruffler attachment on your sewing machine—without ruffling, moisten the edge of the fabric slightly. Before putting ruffler away, remove any moisture by drawing a piece of soft dry cloth through it.

■ Shape seam tape to fit a curve before sewing it in place. Lay tape on the ironing table and steam press it to shape.

■ To make eyelets in a belt for your dress or skirt, use the smallest buttonhole setting or disc on your sewing machine.

■ Turn a narrow tubing of cloth right side out with the help of a rubber-tipped bobby pin. Sew the bobby pin to one end of tubing and pull it through the tube.

■ Before hemming a toddler's play dress, an Illinois mother sews an inch tuck with large machine stitches, just below the hemline. The tuck doesn't show when the hem is finished. It can be let down when the youngster grows and the skirt needs lengthening.

■ When making a rolled hem, put a row of machine stitching along the edge to be rolled. Trim edge close to the stitching. Speeds up the handwork and prevents stretching.

■ Use long pin curl clips to hold a hem in place if material will show pinholes.

■ Cut an extra ⅝" seam allowance on the lower edge of a bodice and the top edge of a skirt when you make a dress for a growing girl. Stitch two waistline seams, ⅝" apart. When extra length is needed, just rip out the first waistline seam.

■ If hard-to-remove creases and stitch marks won't come out with steam pressing, use a wet cloth over a dry one. Press the wet cloth with the iron on dry setting. Hold the iron in place for a few seconds, move it slowly to a new position, hold for a few seconds, etc. Then lift the top cloth and finish pressing until the second cloth is dry. Repeat the process if necessary.

For stubborn creases, use the two cloths as directed. When you have created steam by pressing the wet cloth, take a flat object (wooden block or folded towel will do) and gently pound the steam into the fabric. Then hold object against fabric for a few seconds until steam is gone.

■ Snaps go on easily if you sew the ball part of each snap on the garment first. Rub these with chalk and press them against the other side of the garment. Chalk will mark position for each corresponding half.

■ Small pieces of Velcro work well as fasteners for doll clothes. Easier than snaps or hooks for young fingers to manipulate. Use this closure for ribbon chokers, too.

■ Stitch the pajama drawstring in men's or boys' pajamas at the center back. This keeps the drawstring from pulling out and getting tangled with other clothes in the washer.

■ When you sew slacks with an elastic waistband, stitch a small folded piece of seam tape on the center back at the waistline. This lets you quickly tell front from back.

■ Run a row or two of elastic thread around the sleeve edge of your bulky knit sweater. This holds the sleeve snugly to your arm.

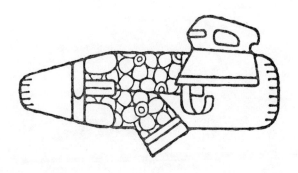

■ Use iron-on tape to hem trousers for a growing boy. When you want to let out the hems, press the tape with a warm iron and it pulls off easily. Takes less time than putting in stitches and ripping them out.

■ Face fabric belts for cotton dresses with iron-on mending tape.

■ Press mending tape to the underside of fabric you use for covering buttons or buckles. This makes the fabric firmer, and you can pull it over the frames without ravels.

■ When tears can't be made inconspicuous with mending tape, let the patches be decorative. Cut a heart, butterfly or flower out of a contrasting color and iron it on top of the tear. Good idea for sports clothes.

■ For maternity use, rip open the center front seam of slacks and skirts a few inches. Attach ties to each side. The waistband will have to be taken off past the center seam, but the loosened piece can be folded back and basted under the section of band still in place. These alterations won't show under a loose topper. Seam and waistband can be restitched after the baby arrives.

■ Fasten a small safety pin at each end of a length of elastic before you insert it in a garment. There's no chance of losing either end; you can feel the pins.

131

■Keep shoulder straps from slipping. Run two or more rows of machine stitching along slip or bra straps at the top of the shoulder, using elastic thread on the bobbin.

Or sew strap holders to the shoulder seams of your dress. Make each holder from a short length of narrow grosgrain ribbon and a snap. The ribbon goes under the slip strap, then snaps against the dress to hold the strap in place.

■Make two sets of straps for sundresses. Sew one set on a bra you wear with the dress; it won't matter if the bra straps show. Good idea for evening dresses with skinny straps, too.

■If you make dresses or tops to wear around the house, buy some extra fabric so you can stitch up aprons to match.

■When you make aprons, sew a small loop of matching fabric under the waistband on the wrong side. Use loop to hang up the apron.

■If your needle gets lodged in heavy fabric or leather when you are sewing by hand, use the shank of your shears as a clamp to pull it through. Most shears provide a good clamp at the point where the handles join the blades.

■To help plastic materials move under the pressure foot without sticking, especially when you topstitch, rub some talcum powder over the stitching area.

∎ You can "baste" plastic materials with paper clips instead of pins or needle and thread. Avoids making holes in the plastic.

∎ Next time you make a blouse for your small daughter, cut it long enough so it can serve as a slip, too. No shirttail to pull out!

∎ To save time when quilting or hemming by hand, thread three or four needles in a row before removing any thread from the spool. Tie one knot to hold the needles on the spool thread. When you begin to sew, measure off the length of thread you need, then cut it behind one needle. Knot the spool thread again to hold other needles in place. When you have used all the needles, stop and thread them again. Your sharp-eyed youngsters may enjoy taking over this job for you.

TRIMMING TIPS

∎ Use rickrack for a scalloped edge finish. Let it ride along the fabric edge; tuck every other point behind the fabric.

∎ When drawing threads from the edge of a fabric to make fringe, crease the fabric or run a thread line to mark the depth of the fringe. Then slash the fabric back to this line, making a slash every few inches and being careful not to cut into the fringe threads. It's easy to stroke out the short lengths with a needle.

133

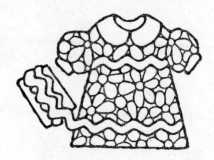

■ Use braid, fringe, rickrack or other trim to cover an old hemline when you lengthen a skirt or dress. Repeat some of the same trim on pockets, yoke, belt or neckline.

This type of trimming also helps coordinate ready-to-wear with homemade garments.

■ Sew different colors of leftover bias tape together for a colorful trim on pot holders, aprons or playclothes.

■ When you use beads for trimming, you may find your needle is too thick for the beads. If so, remove the needle and place a little melted wax on the end of the thread. Twist thread with your fingers until it has a point. When wax is hard, use it for the beads. Nail polish will serve the same purpose.

■ Make a decorative hem for towels, napkins or blouses by winding three-strand embroidery floss, metallic thread or buttonhole-weight thread on your sewing machine bobbin. Loosen the machine tension slightly and lengthen the stitch. Thread the machine as you usually do and stitch with the wrong side of fabric up. This puts the decorative thread on the right side of the fabric.

■ Use your sewing machine to give dresses and aprons a trim that looks like smocking, but takes less time. First, make five parallel rows of gathers (about ¼" apart) on the sewing machine to shirr fabric. Next, wind embroidery cotton on a bobbin, and use it to stitch up and down over the gathers to form Vs. (Stitch Vs with wrong side of fabric up; embroidery cotton is on the right side.) Sew another row of Vs to complete the diamonds.

REPAIRS AND MAKE-OVERS

• Press-on interfacing can be used for patching. It's especially good for lightweight shirts and sheets since it's not so stiff as regular iron-on tape.

• Use iron-on patches to mend garments when a button has been pulled out, tearing the fabric. Cut a slit to the center of the patch. Fit patch around button and iron it on; patch won't show when garment is buttoned.

• Mend a small tear in an umbrella with matching iron-on tape. Place tape on underside and iron.

• Repair gripper snaps that no longer grip tightly. With a small screwdriver, pry up around the center rim of the flat half of the snap so other half will fit more snugly into the opening.

• A marble makes a mini darning egg when you mend tiny holes in glove fingers.

• You can replace lost collar stays with small pieces of pipe cleaner.

- Use pinking shears to cut patches for work shirts or playclothes; you don't have to turn under the edges. Firm fabrics won't fray.

- Reinforce underarm of a kimona sleeve by stitching seam binding into the seam.

- To darn a hole in a flimsy curtain, put a piece of white paper under the hole and make a darn on the sewing machine. Run stitching back and forth. When the curtain is laundered, the paper will dissolve.

- Mend lace collars or insertions by basting net of the same color to the underside. On the right side, sew lace to net with small invisible stitches, following the lace pattern.

- Dip broken shoelace tips into clear nail polish and allow them to harden. The new tips will last as long as the laces.

- Reinforce soles of cloth slippers with iron-on tape for longer wear.

- Make a patchwork housecoat by using an old housecoat turned inside out as a base. Cover the base with patchwork. Feather-stitch the seams with thread in a bright color; do this trim by hand or by machine.

- You can combine two baby blankets to make a larger child's blanket. Trim the two blankets to the same size, then cut each into four rectangular pieces. Arrange pieces alternately in

"My husband insisted a dark blue shirt was worth patching, so I cut out 15 red hearts, assorted sizes, and appliquéd them over the 15 holes. He laughed—but never wore the shirt where someone might see it. P.S. He never again made mending suggestions."

a checkerboard pattern. Lap edges ¼" and stitch. Conceal seams with bands of satin blanket binding 1½" wide, and topstitch over the seams. Finish outside edges with binding.

■ If ready-made dresses with too-short sleeves are a problem, try this. Buy jacket dresses, then transfer the jacket sleeves to the dress. From the original dress sleeves, cut fitted facings for armholes of the sleeveless jacket. If jacket sleeves are a bit full for the dress, use the dress sleeve as a pattern for a better fit.

SOMETHING FOR THE HOUSE

■ If you use bed sheets to line wide draperies, there are fewer seams to sew.

■ When making curtains or draperies, finish the top hems and hang them on rods. Let the curtains stretch a few days, then pin up the bottom hems. If hems are sewn by hand, curtains will not have to be taken down. Ironing table and iron can be brought in to press the hems as you work.

■ Make hot pads for large platters and casseroles by slipcovering magazines. Use fabrics that match or contrast with your table linens or place mats. Snap or baste one side shut, so cover can be removed for laundering. You can add a trim with embroidery, appliqué, stencil —or by quilting the top fabric.

■ If you have tried to pour shredded foam from a package into a pillow cover, you know the foam is difficult to control. It helps to use a No. 3 can with top and bottom removed. Leave an opening in the pillow cover just large enough to insert the can, then put the shredded foam through the can with a large cooking spoon. Use a small can to stuff toy animals with foam or sawdust.

■ When handling shredded foam, rub fabric softener on your hands and arms so the foam won't stick to you.

■ Make sofa pillow covers without zippers or fasteners. Cut the backs in two pieces, wide enough to overlap each other several inches at the center when hemmed. Pillows can be slipped out when covers need washing.

■ You can substitute two short zippers (type used for neckline or skirt) for a long one when you slipcover a cushion. Place zippers so the open ends meet in the center—you pull tabs in opposite directions.

■ To anchor a mattress pad so it won't hump in the middle or slide out of place, stitch a piece of elastic across each corner—about 6″ from the corner. Slip elastic loop under the mattress; loop should fit taut to hold the pad in place.

Or sew a mattress pad onto a worn contour sheet to make a fitted mattress pad.

NEEDLEWORK

▪ When you knit or crochet, use light-colored needles with dark yarn and dark-colored needles with light yarn. It's easier to count the stitches and helps you avoid eyestrain.

▪ Buy your knitting needles in two colors of the same size. Keeping track of pattern rows is easier when they're on different colored needles.

▪ Wind a ball of yarn around the printed skein wrapper. Then if you need to reorder yarn, you'll have the correct information.

▪ To splice yarn neatly for your knitting, thread a darning needle with yarn from a new ball, then run needle (and yarn) through several inches of the yarn you have been working with. Remove needle; pull and straighten yarn to tighten the spliced place. It should be smooth and inconspicuous.

▪ Before crocheting an edge around scarf ends or pillowcases, unthread your sewing machine needle and lengthen the stitch; then stitch around fabric edge. This makes evenly spaced holes through which to crochet.

▪ Keep a spring-type clothespin in your knitting bag. When you stop knitting, clamp needles together with the pin. This keeps stitches from slipping and holds the knitting in proper position.

■Make a tiny embroidery hoop for your dainty work with a metal fruit jar ring. A rubber band will hold the cloth over the ring.

■If raveled yarn is full of kinks, wind it around a glass jar as you unravel it. Dip jar in warm water and allow yarn to dry. It will be soft and usable.

■When a knitting pattern calls for two strands of yarn, run the strands through an empty spool before casting stitches on your needle. Spool keeps yarns from tangling.

■Use a pipe cleaner to hold your knitting stitches in place when you have to remove knitting needles. Ends of pipe cleaner can be bent back, so stitches won't slip off.

■Store all your crochet hooks in a plastic toothbrush container so you can find them.

■Fasten spare strands of wool onto the back of a piece of needlepoint when you complete it. Then the identical wool will be available for any needed repairs, perhaps 15 years after you finish the piece.

■To join new material when crocheting or braiding a rag rug, cut a buttonhole in the end of the strip attached to the rug and another in the end of the strip to be joined. Pull the attached strip through the buttonhole in the new strip. Then pull the opposite end of the new strip through the buttonhole in the attached strip. Pull tightly to form a knot. Saves sewing the pieces together.

- After you've made braids for a rug, sew the braids together with a huge needle made from an old toothbrush. Break off the brush and sharpen the broken end. The hole in the other end of the handle carries the cotton for sewing the braids together.

- Plastic or paper bags make handy containers for hooked-rug strips. Put a different color in each bag, stand bags in a box.

- Attach a drapery hook or cup hook to your rug-hooking frame for holding scissors.

- If you do patchwork, keep the edges of your cardboard patterns from wearing out by coating them with shellac or nail polish before you mark around them.

- Appliqué designs of washable fabric pieces will stay in place for stitching if you use starch to hold them in place. Spread—or spray—a thin coating of starch on the back of each piece. Put the piece in position, cover with a dry cloth and press with a warm iron until the piece is dry. Starch will come out in the first wash.

"Do something creative. You can hook a rug, stitch a picture or knit an afghan—and watch TV at the same time. And you can take forever; needlework looks creative just lying around."

"I knew that motherhood would be a round-the-clock job, but I didn't realize that I'd relinquish my subconscious mind until I tied double knots in my own shoelaces."

Children & Pets

Children & Pets

When little ones arrive,
you learn to cope and compromise

Children put a definite stamp on your house
and life the minute they join the family. They
are a joy, even though their energy and antics
sometimes drive you up the wall. They can be
funny, too, and it helps to keep your sense of
humor working—especially when something
goes wrong. Look for the light side; today's
accident may be tomorrow's laugh.

One mother says she keeps a diary of family happenings, with emphasis on the funny
things. Why not copy the idea? Record such
items as: "Rich stuffed his ears with paper—
so they wouldn't get dirty and have to be
washed," or "Katie picked up the cupcakes I
had decorated for her class party, then
promptly tripped and fell on top of them."

It isn't all laughs, of course. You often feel
pushed and wonder how you spent your time
before a baby arrived. And you learn to cope.
You find ways to arrange your house, time,
work and life-style to accommodate husband,
children and you.

LET THE KIDS HELP

When your toddler wants to help clean house,
let him—before he separates the idea of play
from work. Youngsters slow you down at first,
but if you always say "no," they'll get dis-
couraged. Then just try to enlist them later!

Children's interests and abilities differ, so
you have to judge the readiness of your child

to handle certain jobs. Here's what a 5-year-old in Wisconsin accomplishes in one day: He lays out the younger children's clothes, feeds the turtle and goldfish and goes to the basement for canned food. He helps scrub the bathroom fixtures and does half the breakfast dishes. Kevin's mother doesn't make him work; she lets him. His interest in a job lasts about 10 to 15 minutes. When he tires and gets sloppy, she suggests something else he might like to do.

▪ Draw the outlines of a plate, silverware and napkin on a paper place mat to help children learn how to set the table.

▪ Don't frown on boys learning to cook. A California mother says letting her small son help in the kitchen paid dividends by the time he was 10. When she had a busy day, he would make his favorite meal of spaghetti and meatballs for the family.

▪ When you assign chores to the children, take a turn yourself at each job. This helps them feel that all the work is important.

▪ Let youngsters draw slips for jobs to be done. Include a "free" slip now and then.

▪ A Utah mother uses an alarm clock when she has a chore for her 6-year-old. The alarm is set for the time the job should be finished. Normally, the little girl tends to dawdle, but

"I yelled, 'Who wads up the hand towel behind the rod so it can't dry?' Peter: 'Not me.' Kirby: 'Not me.' Ted: 'It can't be me. I always put it on the floor.' Just try staying mad after that."

she loves to beat the clock. She hurries along to finish the task.

- Hand puppets encourage youngsters to help with the dusting. Make duster puppets from old white cotton socks; draw faces with colored marking pens.

- A Wisconsin mother saves trading stamps to reward her children for doing jobs. They all have stamp books and choose things they want in the catalog. They even ask for extra work to speed the filling of books.

- Every month a Minnesota mother gives each of her youngsters one dollar in nickels. She charges a penalty (one nickel) every time she has to pick up after someone; they get to keep what's left at the end of the month. This system encourages the children to be neat— and saves her time.

REARRANGE THE HOUSE

You can make the house more convenient for the children and yourself if you add, change or modify some of the household fixtures and furnishings. For instance, put rods in a youngster's closet and clothes hooks near the back door at a height he can reach. The closet rod can be an extra one; let it move up as your child grows taller.

If you don't want the extra rod, consider putting a towel rack low on the closet door.

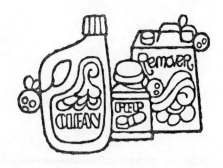

■ Attach a small bell to medicines or other dangerous chemicals. Hold it in place with transparent tape or string. Even though you try to keep poisons out of reach, the bell is a good safety measure. You are alerted in time to prevent accidents.

■ A mite-height mirror in the bathroom is convenient for small children. It works wonders in getting them to brush teeth, wash faces and comb hair.

■ If your toddler likes to play with the telephone, put a wide rubber band around the entire phone to hold the contact points down. It's easy to slip the band to one side when you want to make a call.

■ With a spring-type clothespin, fasten a hand towel to the rod in the bathroom. This enables a small child to wipe his hands without pulling the towel down. Otherwise, the towel ends up in a heap on the floor or draped over the tub. If you can keep the towel hanging, it gets a chance to dry.

■ Designate one drawer for odds and ends, and use it for things you find around the house. Everyone knows where to look for a lost item. Meanwhile, it's out of sight.

■ Add a small dab of red paint or nail polish to hot water faucets. This helps young children avoid burns.

■ Use paint to divide a closet that two teen-age daughters must share. Choose two colors from the room, then paint half the inside wall one color (maybe blue) and the other half the second color (maybe white). Paint hangers for each section to match. This avoids arguments about who takes the most space.

■ Paint the drawers of a chest different colors to help a child identify where to put his clothes. Or let a variety of colors personalize drawers if several children share one chest.

■ Keep small plastic containers of mild liquid detergent in the bathroom, kitchen and laundry room for quick hand-washing. One squirt and you have instant suds—fine for children who won't take time to use a cake of soap. Buy the economy-size container; use it to refill the smaller ones.

■ A table for pickups near the door avoids last-minute confusion on busy mornings. It can hold school books, lunches, library books to be returned, shoes to be repaired and collection envelopes for church.

■ Insert a yardstick through a line of kitchen drawer handles—so your curious toddler can't open the drawers and strew their contents over the floor. It's easy to remove the yardstick when you want to get at a drawer, and you won't have to keep saying "no."

"If you like to read, do it aloud while you rock the baby. She won't know what you are saying, but you'll be talking to her. It's better than a lullaby."

148

■Create a private art gallery for the crayon drawings your children make at school or home. Fasten a piece of cloth to a section of the wall in your kitchen or family room; tape pictures to the cloth. The proud artists can admire their work and show it to friends. When new pictures arrive, change the exhibit.

A length of clothesline along a wall also can be used to display children's art. Use spring-type clothespins to hold pictures.

You even can have an art gallery for a toddler. Tape colored pictures of babies, dogs and cats to the lower part of his clothes closet door—at the youngster's eye level. Change pictures often.

■Try a code system of messages for children instead of leaving notes tacked to the door. A California family uses colored thumbtacks. If Mother puts a blue thumbtack on the door, the children know she will be home soon after they return from school. A red thumbtack tells them she will be late and they should set the table for supper. Casual callers don't know how long she'll be away.

ESPECIALLY FOR BABY

■When your baby is small, keep a calendar in the kitchen. Each time a "first" occurs (first word or tooth, for instance), jot it down. You have a record of your child's growth.

"One of the best inventions is the playpen. This enables me to take out the garbage or bring in garden things and know the baby is all right. Also, when he has climbed into and on top of everything, and my nerves are wearing thin—into the playpen with him!"

149

■ Recipe file cards are fine for recording family medical histories. Start when each child is a baby; list illnesses, dates of vaccinations and shots and any other vital information. The card system seems easier than keeping a book; if you make a mistake, you can replace the card. When a child leaves home, his medical record can go with him.

■ Place a rubber pad in the seat of a very young baby's high chair to keep him from scooting down in the chair when you feed him.

■ A long piece of cellulose sponge in the pocket of a baby's plastic bib will hold the pocket open and absorb spilled milk.

■ To simplify a toddler's bath, hook an inexpensive car seat (with plastic upholstery) over the side of the tub. This is safe and convenient, and it helps keep you dry. Afterward, the seat can drip-dry before you store it.

■ Use a plastic baby carrier to help you bathe a baby who is too big for his own tub and too small for the bathtub. Remove vinyl pad and strap the baby in the chair. You can adjust chair to several positions for convenience.

■ When giving children baths, run a little cold water through the faucet after you fill the bathtub. This helps prevent burns if children touch the faucet.

■ Turn a decorative pot holder into a nursery pincushion. Hang it on a wall near the crib or dressing table; it's a good place to put safety pins when you change diapers.

■ Cover a baby's shoes with discarded socks while he's in the crawling stage. If socks don't have elastic tops, use rubber bands to keep them on. (Best if rubber bands rest against shoe.) Saves many a polishing job.

■ Secure a baby's crib blanket with metal shower-curtain hooks. Sew bone rings to the blanket edges; slip metal hooks through these rings and snap around the side slats of the crib. Hooks will slide up and down the slats, giving the baby room to move and turn—but he won't lose his blanket.

■ Set your young child in front of a mirror when you fix his hair. He'll be interested in watching and will hold still longer.

■ Put bottles of formula in a soft drink carton to store them in the refrigerator. They're easy to move, won't tip over. Carton is a good bottle tote for travel, too.

MEALTIME

■ Fill a large kitchen-style salt shaker with sugar for children to shake on cereal. It's easier for them to handle—and less messy—than dipping spoonfuls from a sugar bowl.

151

■ Warm baby food in aluminum measuring cups—the nested kind. Place food in the 1/3-cup size and set in the 1/2-cup measure, in which you have water to heat. Makes a tiny double boiler that is easy to wash.

Or use an egg poacher if you have one. Each section holds a small quantity and all the food can be steamed at once.

If the oven is in use, you can heat the baby's food in a muffin pan.

■ To keep a 2-year-old from setting his milk glass too near the edge of the table, give him a special coaster with a favorite animal picture on it. This encourages him to set the glass on the coaster after each sip.

■ When you pack lunches in paper bags for children, write their names on the outside with a felt-tipped pen. For a conversation piece at lunchtime, add a motto or famous quotation. Or mention a historical date, such as "Today is the birthday of William Henry Harrison, 9th President of the United States."

■ Include a damp paper towel for sticky fingers when you pack school lunches. Tuck towel in a plastic bag.

■ Getting school lunches together is easy when you put all the essentials on the kitchen table Sunday night and have each lunch-carrier make his sandwiches for the week. Put sandwiches in bags and initial them, then store in the freezer.

Saves time, and there's only one cleanup each week.

■ After-school snacks are the rule at an Ohio home—as soon as the children have changed into playclothes. The rule encourages a quick change and keeps school outfits neat.

■ When your child is too hungry to wait 20 minutes before mealtime, give him his salad to eat—instead of a cookie or candy. This curbs his hunger pangs and encourages him to eat greens and raw vegetables he might skip at the dinner table.

■ Keep a small supply of paper plates in the glove compartment of your car. They're handy if you stop at a drive-in restaurant.

■ A Nebraska mother takes a large cookie sheet for each child when the family eats at a drive-in. The "lap trays" hold the food and protect the upholstery.

■ Carry a snap-type sweater clip to transform a napkin into a bib for a toddler.

■ When a Kansas family dines at a cafeteria, the parents agree to pay for all the food the children eat. The children pay for all the food they take, but don't eat. This teaches the youngsters not to waste food or money.

■ For restaurant eating, a Washington State family sets a price each person can spend.

"Run a test on lunches you pack for children—or anyone. Prepare an identical lunch for yourself, keep it at room temperature until noon, then eat it. You may find there is need for improvement."

153

If someone wants a special salad or dessert, he pays the additional amount. With this system children are conscious of costs.

CLOTHING

▪ Before taking off to buy new clothing for a baby, draw an outline of some well-fitting garments on a large piece of paper. This makes it easy to check garments for size, saves wear and tear on you and the baby.

▪ Write the date of purchase, height and weight of your children on the size tags when you remove them from new clothes. The information will be helpful for future shopping.

▪ Some matching mother-and-daughter aprons solved the problem of "I won't wear a bib" with a Wisconsin 6-year-old.

▪ Cut a piece of clear plastic the length and width of a baby's folded diaper. Slip this liner in next to the last layer of cloth in the diaper. It's cheaper than tailored panties; a yard of plastic makes several liners.

▪ Make thread loops (like belt carriers) on the shoulders of a toddler's shirt to hold his pants' straps in place. With a double thread, form a long loop, then cover the loop with blanket stitches. Run straps through the loops before fastening them.

■ Apply a simple design of colorful self-adhesive plastic tape to your child's rubbers and boots. He'll be able to find them fast in the after-school shuffle.

You also could use plastic cut-outs originally intended to make bathtubs less slippery. Or initial the boot toes with paint.

■ Pull large wool socks over your children's shoes before putting on boots. Socks help to keep snow out, and feet stay warm.

■ Sew a loop of elastic thread inside each cuff of your small child's sweater. Slip loops over his thumbs when putting on his coat—keeps sweater sleeves from pushing up.

■ To prevent a child's scarf from being lost, sew a loop of tape inside the back of the coat collar. Put scarf through the loop.

■ Help your youngster keep his mittens with his coat by sewing a button to each mitten cuff—buttons that will fit in the coat's front buttonholes. When mittens are pulled off, they can be buttoned to the coat.

Or have mittens button to the coat sleeve. For this, make button loops of elastic thread and stitch them on the outside edge of the mitten cuffs. Then sew buttons at corresponding places inside the coat sleeves.

■ Use empty plastic egg cartons to keep children's socks orderly in drawers.

■ Give extra life to your son's worn, not-so-white T-shirts. Dye them a color—or try tie-dying them if you feel ambitious.

■ Make plastic mittens for children to wear over woolen mittens. When youngsters play in the snow, their hands will stay dry and warm.

■ Hang dresses for a little girl on multiple skirt hangers. Clip dresses at the shoulders. One hanger takes six dresses, saves space.

■ Replace a worn-out jacket lining with a boy's shirt (denim or corduroy). Remove collar and cuffs and turn shirt inside out. Slip shirt inside jacket, turn edges under and stitch in place. Children love the inside pockets.

■ You can make mittens from an old sweater. Put the child's hand into the wrist end of the sleeve, with little finger along the seam; sweater cuff becomes mitten cuff. Mark shape of hand, generously, with chalk. Baste around chalk line. Machine stitch ¼" outside basting, using small stitch. Machine stitch again, just inside first stitching. Cut mitten close to outside stitching. Turn and stitch to make a ⅛" French seam.

■ Make some hobo-style pajamas for your youngsters by cutting the pattern pieces from different leftover fabrics. Add some trim to tie the different colors and prints together.

"Children don't have to look spiffy when playing and having fun. If they're happy, what do you care if people notice a hole in the knee? (The seat is another story.)"

- When children are dressed up to go visiting, you might take along some coveralls—in case the youngsters have occasion to play outdoors. Coveralls that are two sizes larger than a child's regular clothing will slip easily over a coat or snowsuit. You won't have to worry about dirt.

- Reinforce the fingertips of your children's mittens with pieces cut from the toes of socks. Turn the mittens wrong side out and slip-stitch portions of the socks in place. This works well since the heels of socks seem to wear out before the toes.

- Keep a little girl's barrette from slipping off her hair by gluing a tiny piece of sponge rubber to the inside of the barrette.

- Before you clean and store the children's winter skirts and trousers, let out the hems. When you wash or dry clean them, lint and soil in the hemline creases are removed. Garments are ready for you to put in new hems when next fall rolls around.

ON THE ROAD

- Take along a rubber sheet to protect furniture when you go visiting with a baby. Handy when you change diapers, too.

- Fill an old handbag or small box with toys and trinkets. These little things will occupy

"There should be time for enjoying children. Now that my son is overseas in uniform, I wonder what household tasks were so important that I couldn't go to his football games. I'm thankful for the ones I did see."

157

children in the car, so you can keep your mind on the driving.

■When you grocery shop with a youngster, let him match products to the coupons you have. This keeps him busy; he doesn't have time to fill the basket with extra items.

■If you wheel a toddler around in a grocery store, tie a small unbreakable toy to the handle of the cart. This keeps him entertained and keeps the toy off the floor.

■Hold a dress rehearsal before your children's first trip to the dentist, as an Arizona family did. The parents examined the youngsters' teeth, using lightweight kitchen utensils as instruments. The children knew what to expect and weren't afraid.

■For travel or camping, an Illinois mother of five boys packs a whole outfit (pants, shirt, underwear, socks) in a plastic bag and writes the child's name on it. The boys easily find their own outfits, and there are no mixed-up clothes. This is helpful when children are close in size.

■For a long car trip, fasten a pocket-style shoe bag to the front seat (bag hangs down in back). The children can use it for crayons, coloring books and small toys. Or carry a baby's essentials in the bag. Pockets hold bottles, thermos, diapers, powder, baby oil.

■Give each child a metal cake pan with a sliding lid to take on a car trip. The pan can hold crayons, coloring books, pencils and paper. When the lid is closed, the child has a writing surface.

Or use cookie sheets as lap trays. Those with raised edges keep crayons under control.

■For a camping or picnic trip, take along a vacuum jug with a spigot. Fill the jug with hot, sudsy water each morning to keep hands and dishes clean.

■Make a list of items that should be packed when a youngster goes away for overnight. This helps the child pack his own bag without forgetting a toothbrush or underwear. Have him pack essentials first, then fill leftover spaces with toys.

■To keep a small child occupied and quiet in church or other gathering, take along a few colored pipe cleaners. These can be twisted into entertaining shapes and make no noise if they are dropped accidentally.

■If your family stays overnight in a motel or look-alike tourist cabins, you can help your children identify the right room. Tie some colorful yarn on the doorknob. Youngsters can't always remember the room number at each stop, but they can spot the bright yarn. When you leave, take the yarn with you to use at the next location.

■Appoint a secretary for your vacation, or let the children take turns at the job. The secretary is responsible for keeping notes about points of interest at places you visit. When you return home, the notes will help you identify slides and arrange pictures and mementos for your scrapbooks.

■When transporting a carload of children, call out "Hands up" before closing the car doors. This command prevents smashed fingers and the children consider it a game.

TOYS IN YOUR LIFE

■Cut sponges to make blocks for preschoolers. When buildings tumble, no one is hurt.

■Shorten the legs of an old card table to make a children's play table.

■Turn an old card table upside down on the floor for your small son's racetrack. Table edges keep his toy autos in bounds, so they won't roll under and into furniture.

■Cut an old tire in half around the circumference and fill one half with water. This circle makes a fine river for sailing tiny boats, and the sailors don't get as wet as when playing in a tub of water.

■Give small children something to work on while you sew. Thread a tapestry needle with

"Cover a cot mattress with heavy denim and give it to the boys for a gym mat. They'll like it for stunts— better than the furniture."

colored twine. (Yarn or heavy thread works, too.) Attach twine to a mesh dishcloth. Children can weave the needle and twine through the mesh.

▪ When stuffing a homemade doll, put a small can containing a few pebbles into its head. A "rattle brain" doll is fun!

▪ Imitation fur coats that are worn out can be turned into wonderful stuffed toys. How about a stuffed toy that's also a pillow?

▪ Old nylon stockings are good for stuffing toys. When washed, toys dry quickly.

▪ Make a sturdy book for a small tot by using the sides of cardboard boxes as pages. Paste colorful pictures on the cardboard surfaces, punch several holes along one end, then lace with stout cord. Leave the cord loose enough so the book opens easily.

▪ For safety, remove the glass eyes from a toddler's stuffed doll. Replace with stitches of thread or embroidery floss.

▪ Before giving youngsters a new box of crayons, place tape over the tuck-in at the bottom. Crayons are less likely to be spilled.

Or transfer crayons to an empty metal box designed to hold adhesive bandages.

▪ Amuse children and teach them numbers by using squares cut from old calendars. Devise

"After I put a coat of paste wax on the floor, the children pull on socks and slide back and forth over the surface. They have great fun—and they do a great buffing job."

your own games. Young children can match all the sevens or eights, for instance. Or see which child can match the most numerals within a certain time limit.

▪ A child's sleigh can be made out of an ordinary sled by cutting off the legs of an old chair just below the seat and fastening the seat to the sled.

▪ Save waxed milk or food cartons and let small children have them for bowling pins. Used with a large hollow ball, they provide a safe indoor game. Rinse the cartons and tape down the tops.

▪ String bags (new, or salvaged from oranges you bought) are handy for storing toys and boots. Hang the bags on low hooks—the children can find what they want since contents are visible. Carry a mesh bag to the beach, too. When it's time to come home, put the toys in the bag and shake them. Most of the sand will be left on the beach.

▪ Keep a small rectangular wastebasket at the end of your kitchen counter to collect toys that toddlers drag into the kitchen—but forget to drag back.

▪ A treasure box of household discards entertains small visitors. Fill a box with old jewelry, ribbons, beads, etc. Let guests take some loot with them when they leave.

■A toy tea set serves useful purposes. When tempers flare or children are restless, suggest a tea party. Fix hot chocolate or fruit juice while the children set the table. The party can last about 45 minutes; it gives the children a rest and restores their good humor. Also, when a toddler balks at his food, a toy cup from the tea set may renew his interest in eating.

■A play box for paper cutting is great for a 4-year-old. Your child will enjoy sitting in a large, shallow box while making paper dolls or snowflakes; box catches the scraps.

■To sharpen a crayon without waste, hold it near heat until softened. Then taper it to a point with your fingers.

■Before children play with the new games they receive as gifts, tape the directions for playing inside the box lid.

■Rotate your child's toys so he has something "new" for play occasionally. Pack a box of toys and store it out of sight. Exchange the contents periodically.

■Use stackable plastic vegetable bins for toy storage. Or store playthings in shallow boxes mounted on casters; they can be rolled under the bed out of the way. Boxes are easily made from plywood or from drawers out of a discarded dresser.

■ An old piano bench makes a fine play table for children when used with low stools or chairs. It has storage space for crayons, drawing paper and games.

■ Put a sponge rubber pad inside your son's wagon for him to kneel on. It will save him painful bumps and help keep the knees of his pants from wearing thin.

■ Place a 4' strip of heavy rubber matting under your youngster's swing. This protects shoes from scuff marks and keeps mud to a minimum after a rain.

■ Pick-up time can be a game for youngsters who have a toy box on wheels. Put casters on a sturdy wooden box so the children can push it around—indoors or out.

■ The perforated basket from an old coffee percolator is a good bath toy for small children. They enjoy scooping up water and watching it run through the holes.

■ Tie an old alarm clock to your child's tricycle or wagon—set to go off when it's time for him to return home. He'll enjoy the game of timing himself, and (hopefully) he'll arrive more promptly for meals.

■ Put a play tent on a wooden platform with wheels attached so it can be moved. This lets the youngsters change their campsite around the yard and keeps them off the ground when it's damp. Later on, you can use the tent to protect summer lawn furniture if your storage space is limited.

■Mark play area boundaries with homemade red flags mounted on sticks and pushed into the grass. This reminds children not to stray.

■Make a safe Halloween jack-o'-lantern for your children. Use a flashlight instead of a candle to light up the features. You can cut a hole in the bottom of the pumpkin to insert the flashlight.

■A plastic cutlery tray helps keep crayons, pencils and scissors in order.

■Caps from toothpaste or shaving cream tubes make flower pots for a dollhouse. Fill cap with modeling clay; stick in a piece of evergreen or a small artificial flower.

■Your child's bicycle basket won't spill its contents when going over bumps if he makes a guard from a doorspring. Attach one end of the spring to an inside corner of the basket. Hook it diagonally across the basket over things that are being carried.

■Protect cyclists by placing reflector tape on bicycle pedals. The moving bits of reflected light help motorists easily spot a rider after dark.

Or you can put small reflector buttons on each bike pedal, placed so they can be seen

"When toys have to be put away, it's happier for all when I help and guide rather than direct and nag."

from the rear. The tiny red lights bobbing up and down attract more attention than the single reflector on the rear fender.

■ Take a pair of earmuffs apart, then fasten the fabric sections to the back wheel hubs of a tricycle. This saves wear and tear on furniture and woodwork during winter months when children play indoors.

■ If your young child rides his tricycle indoors, teach him to be careful. Attach a license plate to his trike and give him a wallet in which to carry his driver's license. Establish driving rules and impound his trike for crashing into a wall or furniture. He will soon learn about obeying the traffic laws of the house.

KIDS DO GET SICK

■ Put a bell by your child's bed when he's sick. One ring means come when you can—two rings mean come right away, please.

■ No bed table for your patient? If you have a sewing machine cabinet with a leaf that extends when opened, let it serve as a table.

■ Use an egg timer when you take a child's temperature. Let the patient hold the timer while the thermometer is in his mouth. The 3 minutes go faster when he can watch the sand trickle through the glass.

■Make a spill-proof drink container for a sick child who needs to take lots of liquids in bed. Sterilize a small mayonnaise jar and its screw lid. Puncture the lid top near the edge and fill the jar with milk or fruit juice. Screw on top and insert a drinking straw.

■A bright new muffin pan is better than a tray for serving meals to a sick child. Put each food in a separate muffin cup, and there will be no dishes to slide. A small glass of milk or fruit juice also may be set into one of the sections.

■To help you remember to give the correct dosage of medicine, count out the number of pills needed for the day. Put them in a small container. At the end of the day, you can easily check if you missed any.

■Before you give a child bitter-tasting medicine, let him hold a piece of ice on his tongue to chill the taste buds.

■When someone is ill, you can protect the mattress with a flannel-backed plastic tablecloth. With the flannel side down, the moisture-proof covering stays in place.

■Make a temporary backrest for a bed patient, using a 22″ length of 1×12″ lumber. Sandpaper rough spots and insert wood between pillow and pillowcase. Prop against headboard.

■Pin a strong paper bag to the side of the mattress so your patient can toss in tissues.

■If your patient's bedroom is a bit chilly, have him slip a cardigan sweater or bathrobe on backward to keep his arms warm.

■When someone in the family has a cold, put a wide, flat rubber band around his drinking glass or cup. You'll find it much easier to keep the glass—and the cold—confined to the original owner.

OH, YES—PETS

■Use old nylon hose to stuff a pillow for a pet dog or cat. The pillow can be washed and dried in a jiffy.

■Keep an extra baster to siphon off refuse that collects in the fish bowl.

■Use a funnel to fill feeding dishes in a bird cage; you can make one of paper. Slide seeds into dishes without spilling.

"Small children have bad days, too. I try to read to them or rock them when these days arrive—because children are more important than any housekeeping chore."

■Try putting a litter of puppies into a baby's discarded playpen when they become too large to keep in a box. Tack screen wire around the bottom to keep them in.

■Make a cat-proof birdbath for your yard. Your main materials are the lid of a garbage can (painted white, if metal) and a length of drain pipe. Plant the pipe upright in the ground. Fasten a sash weight by wire from the handle at the center of the lid. Hang weight down through the pipe—to anchor the birdbath to its base. If a cat jumps onto the birdbath, his weight will tilt the rim, upsetting the rascal.

■ Give the birds a real treat by pouring fat drippings over stale bread crumbs before putting crumbs out in the yard.

■ You can borrow the pulley clothesline idea for hanging a bird feeder. It's easy to pull the feeder to the back door for replenishing, no matter how bad the weather. The birds are safe while they feed, and feed is safe from any marauders.

■ Don't forget a holiday feast for the birds. Mold cakes of seed and melted suet in small containers. While mixture is soft, insert a pipe cleaner to use as a hanger.

■ If you are continually vacuuming up dog hairs around the house, there's probably an odor build-up in the vacuum. Put some moth balls in the vacuum case to banish it.

"One day as I was cleaning house, my 3-year-old son asked, 'Mom, do you want me to clean while you play?'"

Game Time

Game Time

*Keep the kids busy and
help the grownups relax*

Every once in a while you need an activity or game to enliven a youngster's birthday party, a bridal shower or a potluck supper. And what about those rainy days when your child is indoors, confined—and restless?

This chapter gives you a collection of activities for one (or more), games for two (or more), games for small groups, action relays and a few quiet quizzes and word games. The chapter is a handy reference for large or small gatherings and for times when your youngster can't think of anything to do—*now!* Try a quiz or word game yourself when you have a minute. It helps you relax, and the answers are there if you need them.

ACTIVITIES FOR ONE (OR MORE)

Here are ideas to keep one child amused. If you use the activity for two or more persons, let the players compete for the fastest time or the highest score.

• *Macaroni spell:* Measure out a cupful of alphabet macaroni. See how many words a player can spell in a given time. For a Christmas party, ask people to spell holiday words, such as *tree, gift, holly, mistletoe* and *turkey.*

• *Jigsaw puzzles:* Turn magazine covers into puzzles. Back a picture with cardboard and cut it into various-shaped pieces. For a small child, cut the picture into a few large sections. Challenge an older child or an adult by cutting the picture into more and smaller pieces.

■ *Copy writers:* Assemble old newspapers, picture magazines, scissors and paste. Have the player clip a startling—or funny—magazine picture; then, under it, have him paste a suitable title that has been cut from one of the newspapers.

■ *Telescope walk:* Stretch a long piece of string on the floor and provide a pair of opera or field glasses. Have the player look at the string through the glasses and try to walk the straight line.

■ *Fireside scavenger:* You can capture the fun of a scavenger hunt without leaving the living room. Furnish old newspapers, magazines, catalogs, etc., that can be cut up. Supply scissors and a list of 10 items that are pictured in the materials. (Describe items in detail, such as woven slipcovers, pink garment bags, a cocker spaniel puppy.) Each item must be found, cut out and presented in order. If several persons do this, first one to finish is the winner.

■ *Telegram fun:* For this game you need old magazines, scissors, paste and paper. Have the player cut single words or phrases from magazine and paste them together to form

"My young space-minded son calls the double boiler a 'two-stage pot.'"

sentences of a telegram. You can suggest the telegram be for a specific purpose—to announce the birth of a baby, explain an absence, announce a visit, send congratulations, ask for money.

■ *Jingles:* On a slip of paper, write two pairs of rhyming words—for example, *June, moon* and *yellow, mellow.* Have player make up jingles using the words.

■ *Your nose knows:* Line up a half dozen or so numbered bottles containing such things as perfume, shaving lotion, vinegar, iodine, etc. Give each player a piece of paper. As he goes down the line of bottles, he can smell each one and write down what he thinks the bottle contains.

GAMES FOR TWO (OR MORE)

■ *Basket bounce:* Place a wastebasket in the center of the room, and mark a line about 8′ from the basket. Have players bounce a ball into the basket from the line. To score, the ball must bounce once before landing in the basket.

■ *Blow straight:* Make a path on a smooth floor or on a long table by laying string in two parallel lines about 12″ apart. The player who blows a Ping-Pong ball the longest distance down the path without touching the string is the winner.

■ *Tumble the tee:* Place golf tees upside down on a table, in bowling-pin position. Have players try to knock down tees by snapping a button (with the edge of another button, tiddlywink-fashion) toward them from a distance of 8". Allow 3 turns per player, and score 1 point for each tee that is upset.

■ *Date toss:* Place a large calendar on the floor, and mark a line 6' away. Give each player 5 checkers.

Players stand on the line and toss for dates. Saturdays and holidays count 5; Fridays and Sundays, 3; other days, 1. Give each player one—or several—turns. Highest score wins.

■ *Ring the bell:* Make a wire hoop 12" to 14" in diameter and suspend a small bell in it. Hang hoop vertically by a string in an open doorway, 5' or 6' feet from the floor.

Each player, in turn, stands 8' to 15' away and throws a small, soft rubber ball through the hoop. Each person gets five tries. Score 10 points if the ball goes through the hoop and 20 points if it goes through without ringing the bell. (Better clear the room of breakables before you start throwing.)

■ *Listen and tell:* On a table, put an assortment of objects—kitchen bowls, large and small glasses, a book, a metal object, large vase, and so forth. Have each player, in turn, watch and listen while you strike each object. Then have him turn his back and try to identify the objects as you strike them. The one who recognizes the largest number is the winner.

▪ *Pin the bottle:* Give each player a large empty jar (mayonnaise jar is fine) and 5 clothespins. The jar, on the floor, is the target for the clothespins which must be held at eye level and dropped into it. The player who drops all his clothespins into his jar first is the winner.

▪ *Penny splash:* Place a glass of water on the floor about 2′ behind a chair. Have players take turns sitting on the chair and tossing pennies behind them to see who can make the most land in the glass. Each player may have 10 turns. No one may turn around to see where he is throwing the penny, but he may take a long look at the position of the glass before he begins to toss. Better play this one in the kitchen, where a few splashes of water won't hurt!

▪ *Juggle the lines:* Type or print several copies of a short story or verse that is familiar to everyone. Paste each copy on lightweight cardboard. Cut the story or verse apart line by line and put each set in a separate envelope. Give each player (or group) an envelope of lines. Have them race to put the lines in order. The fastest to put line in order wins.

■ *Blowout:* Here's another version of musical chairs. Arrange chairs in a circle, facing in, with a large space in the middle of the room. All but one player—the narrator—has a chair and is seated. The narrator whispers the name of an auto part to each person. Then he starts walking within the circle, telling an original story of an imaginary auto ride. As he mentions each part of the car, the player having that name gets up and follows him, forming a line.

The story continues until most of the chairs are empty. Then the narrator says, "And then we had a blowout." At the word "blowout" all the players, including the narrator, race for the chairs. The person failing to get a seat is then "It." He becomes the narrator and starts another story.

This game can be varied by giving the players flower names and telling a story of a walk through the garden; use a different *key* word. Or use the names of animals for a trip through the zoo.

■ *Pinups:* Pile up as many sheets of paper as there are players. Toss 12 kernels of corn on the top, and where they fall, prick holes through the pile with a long pin. Then hand out a sheet to every player. Each player draws any figure he wishes, using all of the holes in the main outline. Have an exhibit; select a winner, if you like.

"I find combining my work with the children's play is rewarding. If I keep them interested in 'I Spy' or a word game as I clean house, they soon say, 'Let me help, Mama.'"

■ *Concentration:* This will test a person's memory. Take a deck of cards and spread it out on a table, cards face down. Players sit around the table. Each player, in turn, picks up 2 cards, one at a time. The aim is to find pairs.

Suppose the first person turns up a 7 and then a 10. They are not a pair, so he turns them down again. Perhaps the next player turns up a jack and then a 3. He turns them down again. The third person turns up his first card; it may be a 7. He knows that another 7 already has been turned up. Can he remember where it is?

If he locates it, he keeps the pair and is entitled to another turn. If he fails to find a pair, he turns both cards down and the next person proceeds. When all the cards have been matched, the person holding the most pairs wins.

■ *Spoon the egg:* For this game you need a hard-boiled egg, an egg cup and a wooden mixing spoon. Have each player try to pick up the egg with the spoon and place it in the cup, pointed end up, without upsetting the cup. He may not touch the egg or cup with his hands. Give each player four turns.

■ *Marble lift:* Give each player 12 marbles in a small cup, a second cup and 2 long pencils. Place the cups about 4″ apart in front of each player, and ask him to lift the marbles from one cup to another with the 2 pencils, chopstick fashion. He may not touch the marbles with anything but the pencils. If a marble drops on the floor, it must be put back into the first cup. First player to finish wins the game.

■ *Glass lift:* Cover 2 similar glasses with napkins, so that no one can see what's in them. Leave one glass empty, and fill the other glass with sand or heavy nails.

Ask someone to lift the glasses, one in each hand, and hold them at the same height as quickly as possible.

You can make a game of it by preparing a pair of glasses for each person, to see who can raise the glasses most evenly in the shortest time.

■ *Circle the pencil:* Hang a finger ring in a doorway at low shoulder level. Give each player a pencil. He must hold the pencil out front at arm's length. Walking from a starting line 10′ from the ring and closing one eye to "aim," he must try to put the pencil through the ring without bending his elbow. Give each player five chances. Score 1 point each time he succeeds.

■ *Color jumble:* Make sticks for this game by coloring round toothpicks as follows: 1 black, 6 blue, 6 green, 12 yellow, 14 red. The first player holds the sticks vertically about an inch above the table, then opens his hand and lets the sticks fall. He then picks up as many sticks as he can, one at a time, without moving another stick. If he moves any other stick but the one he's trying to pick up, he loses his turn, and the next player tries. If he picks up all sticks, he starts the game over. It's like jackstraws. The black stick is the only one which can be used as a helper.

Score as follows: black, 10 points; blue, 5; green, 3; yellow, 2; red, 1. Play for a 200-point score.

■ *Baffling cards:* Take 10 cards of any suit from a deck; use the ace to the ten. Arrange cards ahead of time. Then lay cards in an even line, face down. Have the ace at the left, then the two, on up to the ten.

Ask someone to transfer any number of cards from the left to the right—one at a time—without otherwise changing the sequence. Tell him you will guess the number of cards he moved. Then turn your back.

When the player says he has made the move, turn over the card at the right end. The number of this card is your answer.

■ *Pan toss:* Cut small pieces of paper or cardboard to fit into the bottoms of a 12-section muffin pan. Number them as follows, starting with the top row of the tin and working across each row, left to right; 10, 5, 8, 7, 9, 6, 4, 1, 11, 12, 3, 2. Place the pan on the floor at one end of the room, and tilt it by placing a book under the end nearest the wall.

Each player, in turn, stands 8' away from the pan and tries to toss 5 pennies into it. To get his score, add the numbers in the sections where his pennies have landed. Player with high total wins. For a prize, award a bag of shiny new pennies.

■ *Hidden talent:* Paste a few pictures from magazines on a paper in strange positions. A person's head, a pair of hands, a pair of feet and a dish of food might be on one paper. Another might have a flower, a bucket, a sink and a hat. Make up one sheet for each player.

At the starting signal have each player complete his picture with pencil lines. The winner may be either the first one finished, or the one who produces the best picture.

GAMES FOR SMALL GROUPS

■ *The model:* Have a girl enter the room wearing many items of clothing and accessories—jacket, boots, gloves, bracelets, hat, collar and so forth. Tell the group to observe her closely.

After parading around the room as a model would do, she leaves. Then ask the guests to list all the items of clothing and jewelry they saw. Score 1 point for each correct item; 1 off for each error.

"I heard one of my boys say to the other, 'One good thing about Mom—it doesn't take much to make her laugh.' What a nice compliment!"

181

■ *Quick plots:* Collect two identical sets of articles, such as toothbrushes, soap, newspaper clippings, ribbons, ticket stubs, etc., and put each set in a paper bag.

Divide your group into two teams, giving each team a bag. Allow 10 minutes for the teams to think up plots involving every article; then teams take turns acting out their stories. Funniest stunt wins.

■ *Paper charades:* Divide the crowd into two teams, and give each a large pad of paper and a pencil. Seat the teams at opposite ends of the dining table, with you, as captain, seated between them.

A messenger from each team goes to the captain, who whispers the name of an object or the title of book, movie or song (same to both players). Back at their places, the messengers draw the subject for their teams. First team to guess what it is gets a point. Team with most points in a half hour wins.

■ *Handshake:* Blindfold one person, and ask him to identify as many other players as he can by shaking hands with them as he walks down the line. Shuffle the line each time a new person is blindfolded. Keep score to see who identifies the most players.

■ *Land that fish:* Cut out 20 or more cardboard fish, and glue a puff of cotton on the head of each. On the other side of each fish, mark a number from 1 to 10. Place fish in a large pan, cotton side up.

Give all players fishing poles, made by tying strings to the end of sticks, 1' long. Add hooks made from bent pins.

Have players catch fish by hooking the cotton. To count scores, total numbers on the fish each player has landed.

■ *Needle race:* Place a bowl of assorted needles and several spools of thread in the center of a table. Divide the players into pairs. Allow each pair 5 minutes to thread as many needles as possible, one person holding the needle, the other a length of thread taken from one of the spools. (Each needle must have a separate length of thread.) After the time is up, ask each couple to remove the threads and replace the needles in the bowl. Couple who threads the most needles wins. (Optional ending: Have the winning pair race each other for the prize.)

■ *Marketing:* "It," the shopper, walks around the room and stops in front of another player. He says, "I'm going to Chicago, what can I buy?" and counts to 10 rapidly. Before he finishes counting, the player he's standing before must name three things that begin with "C." If the player can't do this, he gives up his seat and becomes "It." Any city can be used, and the objects to be bought must begin with that city's initial.

■ *Mother Goose bee:* Choose two teams and have players line up as they would for a spelling bee. Instead of spelling words, give each person the first line of a nursery rhyme and ask him to supply the second line. The team that can supply the most second lines wins.

■ *Cake batter:* Place chairs in a circle, one less than the number of players. When players (the "batter") are seated facing the center, the one who's left standing acts as cook and goes to the center of the circle. The cook stirs the "batter" by calling orders, "left," "right," "right," "left," in any sequence. The players must shift seats according to the orders. When he calls "across the bowl," players must move to chairs on the opposite side of the circle. The cook should call directions slowly enough to give the players time to change chairs, but fast enough to cause confusion. Now and then he tries to get into the "batter." When he succeeds, the player without a seat is the new cook.

■ *Stick 'em up:* If the boys think they know the girls pretty well, have all the girls stand behind a screen and show just their hands. Let the boys identify them. No jewelry allowed.

■ *Fashion foibles:* Here's a chance to let everyone try his hand at fashion illustrating. Ask someone to look at a fashion illustration in a magazine and describe to the others the fashion in detail, mentioning the ruffles, the bows, the buttons, and so on. As he talks, everyone else tries to draw the object from his description. Then have an exhibit! Or, choose the best illustration and give a prize.

■ *Picture this:* Divide group into pairs and seat partners back to back. Give one person in each pair a pencil and paper. Supply the other with some item familiar to everyone—an egg beater, a flag, a clock.

Without telling his partner what it is, the one holding the object describes it while his partner draws it. The pair with the most recognizable picture wins.

■ *Blindfold hurdles:* Make the loser from another game be "It" to do this one. Line up a row of large food jars or similar objects on the floor. Then have "It" walk down through them, stepping over each one. When he gets to the end, blindfold him, turn him around, and send him back over the hurdles. But while one person is turning him, quickly remove all the jars.

"It's more fun for children to make a mess than to clean it up. That's where your good, orderly example comes in. Help them pick up and put away until they get the habit."

■ *Name bingo:* For a good mixer, make a card for each guest, and rule it off like a bingo card. Fill in the squares with your guests' initials, arranged in a different order on each card. Pass out the cards, and instruct guests to get signatures in the squares to correspond with the initials. First to fill a complete line, up and down, crosswise or diagonal, yells "Bingo!" and wins.

■ *Fun with sayings:* Send one player out of the room. Then choose a saying and give each remaining player one word from it. (Repeat words, if necessary.) When "It" returns, he begins to ask questions; a player must use his special word each time he answers. "It" tries to guess the saying.

Suppose the saying is "Make hay while the sun shines." The question, "How are you today?" might be answered, "I'd feel better if the sun would come out," by the person whose word is "sun." Or "I ate some hay this morning and have an upset stomach," if his word is "hay."

■ *Clothesline circles:* With a 4′ piece of clothesline or heavy string, make a circle on the floor. Cross the ends where they meet to make the circle and pull on them in opposite directions so that the circle gradually becomes smaller. Ask each player in turn to tell you to stop when the circle has reached the size of his waist. Measure. Best guesser wins.

■ *Amateur artists:* Select magazine advertisements, preferably those with people, and cut them in half. Paste them on paper. Distribute the half pictures with pencils, and ask each person to complete his picture. You should have a humorous exhibit.

■ *Missing clue:* Choose a "detective," and ask him to sit in a chair in the center of the room. Have a blindfold ready.

Bring from hiding a tray of 10 clues such as a pencil, piece of newspaper, glove, knife, glass, bottle of medicine. Let the detective study the tray for a few seconds.

Now blindfold him, and have someone take away and hide one clue. Remove the blindfold and give the detective 30 seconds to decide which object is missing. If he fails, the person who removed the clue becomes the next detective. He keeps the position until he fails.

■ *High steppers:* Tie a blown-up balloon to the ankle of each player. The idea is to break the balloons of others, but keep your own from being broken. This is as much fun to watch as it is to play.

■ *Active anagrams:* Each person wears a large card tied around his neck with string. A big letter is printed in crayon on each card. Give the players letters that are most commonly used in words.

When the scorekeeper says "Go!" everybody tries to join one or more other players to spell out a word. When a group forms a word, they go to the scorekeeper, who gives each player in the word 1 point. Then they separate and try to form new words. Player with the most points wins.

■ *Who's the leader?* First of all, decide who is to be "It," and send him from the room. The other players decide who is to be the leader. "It" returns and finds all the players performing the same movement, maybe swinging their other players decide who is to be the leader. quietly starts another motion, such as twisting his head; the others quickly imitate him. If the leader is identified, he becomes "It."

■ *Grandmother went to Paris:* This is an old, old favorite with people of all ages. All the players sit in a circle, and the leader starts the game by saying "Grandmother went to Paris and took an apple," The next player says "Grandmother went to Paris and took an apple and a banana." The sentence goes round and round the circle, each player repeating all the articles mentioned before and adding one of his own, but the articles must be in alphabetical order. If a player forgets an article, or puts it in the wrong place, he is out of the game.

■ *Animal crackles:* Write out a list of animal actions, such as: Birds fly, Toads hop, Dogs bark, Mules kick, Snakes hiss. Include some false actions, like: Cats fly, Fish growl, Chickens swim.

Players stand in a circle around the leader, who reads the list. Everyone must instantly follow the directions, unless the directions are false. Those who obey the false directions are out.

Leader reads fairly fast, to catch the players. A helper could watch for mistakes. Last person in circle wins.

ACTION RELAYS

■ *Pass key:* Choose two teams and have players on each team stand side by side, linking hands. Give a key to the first person in each line. The object is to pass the key down the line without unclasping hands. If the key is dropped, it must be picked up, with all hands still clasped.

■ *Pick up:* Choose two teams; give each a pair of big gloves and a cup with 6 pieces of uncooked macaroni. Each team leader carries his cup to a goal, empties the macaroni, then returns it to the cup—one piece at a time—wearing the gloves. He then gives the equipment to the next team member who takes a turn. Team to finish first wins.

■ *Orange roll:* Choose two teams, and supply each with a pencil and an orange. Mark starting and goal lines. The first member of each team rolls the orange along the floor to the goal line, pushing it only with the pencil. There, he turns and rolls it back to the next player, who repeats the roll. First team to finish wins.

"Parties that are most fun for the kids probably are the most fun for Mother, too."

189

▪ *Gumdrop race:* Choose two teams; have each form a line 5′ from a table. On the table, put toothpicks and paper cups (one cup per person), each filled with 6 gumdrops. At a signal, the first person in each line rushes to the table and picks up a toothpick and a cup. He returns to feed the gumdrops, speared one at a time with the toothpick, to the second person. Then the second person takes a turn and feeds the third person, and so on. Last person feeds the first in line. First team to finish wins.

▪ *Feather fun:* Here's an indoor race that doesn't take a lot of room or break anything. Give each player a plate with 5 feathers on it. At a signal, players carry plates across the room without touching the feathers. If feathers flutter off, the player must stop, pick them up, and put them back on the plate. The first player to reach the finish line with all feathers on his plate is the winner. Last one can be "It" for another game. Or form teams; first team to finish is winner.

▪ *Fire brigades:* Choose two teams of "firemen" and have them line up. Give each team a bucket and a pile of identical articles. Include some hard-to-pick-up things, such as beans, thumbtacks, paper clips and stamps.

At the "go" signal, the first in line places one article in the bucket, which is then passed quickly down the line. The last "fireman" in the line removes the article and places it on the "fire" (a chair). Then he runs with the bucket to the front of the line, puts in another article, and passes the bucket down the line again.

The winner: First team to move all its articles and "put out the fire."

■ *Squeeze through:* Make two circles of heavy elastic just big enough to slide over a person's body. Choose two teams. Have first member of each team race to a goal, slide through the elastic, then return to end of line. The next member in line makes his run, etc. First team to finish wins.

■ *Walking numbers:* Choose up equal teams of 10 players or less. Supply each person with a number to hang on his back. Use large cardboards on which the figure from 0 to 9 have been heavily marked—an identical set for each competing team.

The leader calls a number, say 2,573, and each team races to present that number. (The leader must call only numbers that can be formed by the groups.) Allow 1 point for the team that first presents the correct number. The team to get 10 points first wins.

QUIZZES

■ *Cake talk:* Have players guess the kind of cake described by each clue. For instance,

what cake grows in an orchard? The answer is
Fruitcake. Here are some other clues:
1. Drink out of this
2. Satan's supper
3. Breakfast beverage
4. Use this in the bathtub
5. Heavenly fare
6. Stands on its head
7. Sixteen ounces
8. A child's plaything
Answers: (1) Cupcake (2) Devil's food
cake (3) Coffee cake (4) Sponge cake
(5) Angel food cake (6) Upside-down cake
(7) Pound cake (8) Marble cake

■ *Gift conundrums:* Here's a gift list all made
out for a family. Can you decide what each person will get?
1. Dad wants a Dalmatian. Will he get (a)
an etching (b) a dog (c) a rare stamp?
2. Mother wants a chatelaine. Is it (a)
jewelry (b) an exotic plant (c) a tapestry?
3. Big brother wants a derringer. Is his
hobby (a) harness racing (b) fishing
(c) target practice?
4. Little brother wants an oboe. Will he get
(a) a musical instrument (b) a motor
bike (c) a model airplane?
5. Big sister will look lovely in her peignoir.
Will she wear (a) a hair ornament (b)
a corsage (c) a negligee?

6. Little sister wants a parrakeet. Is it (a) a bird (b) a monkey (c) a horse?
7. Aunt Sue's hobby is ceramics. Will you give her (a) antique pewter (b) pottery (c) carved jade?
8. Uncle Joe gets a niblick. Will he use it (a) golfing (b) bowling (c) playing polo?
9. Grandmother will enjoy an ottoman. Will she (a) hang it on the wall (b) put her feet on it (c) put flowers in it?
10. Grandfather gets a meerschaum in his stocking. Is his gift (a) a knitted jacket (b) a walking stick (c) a pipe?

Answers: (1) b (2) a (3) c (4) a (5) c (6) a (7) b (8) a (9) b (10) c

■ *Flag facts:* True or false?
1. Our Flag is the only red-white-blue one.
2. There have never been more than 13 stripes in the Flag.
3. The 13 stripes honor patriots of 1776.
4. To signify mourning, the Flag is flown at half-mast.
5. To display the Flag with the stars down is a signal of defeat.

Answers: (1) False. Great Britain and several other nations have red, white and blue flags. (2) False. In the War of 1812 our Flag had 15 stripes. (3) False. They are in honor of the 13 original states. (4) True. (5) False. It is a signal of distress.

"When I surprise my daughter with freshly baked cookies, she gratefully presents me with a mud pie."

193

■ *Take a number:* Below is a list of expressions, proverbs, titles and common sayings, each containing one or more numbers. How many can you fill in?

1. —— for the money, —— for the show.
2. —— Coins in the Fountain.
3. —— a couple, —— a crowd.
4. A Tale of —— Cities.
5. —— a loaf is better than none.
6. —— peas in a pod.
7. A stitch in time saves ——.
8. —— Blind Mice.
9. —— come ——.
10. —— Frenchmen can't be wrong.
11. The first —— years are the hardest.
12. —— and —— blackbirds baked in a pie.
13. What this country needs is a good —— cent cigar.

Answers: (1) One, two (2) Three (3) Two's, three's (4) Two (5) Half (6) Two (7) Nine (8) Three (9) Seven, eleven (10) Fifty million (11) Hundred (12) Four, twenty (14) Five

■ *Which way?* How did these folks go?
1. Cinderella went to the ball in a (a) coach (b) surrey (c) carriage.
2. Yankee Doodle went to town on a (a) mule (b) donkey (c) pony.
3. Huckleberry Finn sailed the Mississippi River on a (a) white sailboat (b) ferryboat (c) raft.

4. Casey Jones reached the Promised Land in a (a) golden chariot (b) airplane (c) locomotive.
5. The owl and pussycat went to sea in a (a) round tub (b) pea-green boat (c) large wooden shoe.
6. Lady Godiva rode through Coventry on a (a) swan (b) camel (c) horse.
7. Eliza crossed the river (a) on foot (b) by dog sled (c) by boat.
8. The Israelites crossed the Red Sea (a) in galley boats (b) on 100 rafts (c) on foot.
9. Lord Byron crossed the Hellespont by (a) rowing (b) sailing (c) swimming.

Answers: (1) a (2) c (3) c (4) c (5) b (6) c (7) a (8) c (9) c

▪ *Arithmetic quiz:* Find the wisest "owl" at the party with this. How many:
1. Feet in a fathom?
2. Pounds in a short ton?
3. Inches in a hand?
4. Square rods in an acre?
5. Cubic inches in a gallon?
6. Yards in a mile?
7. Dozen in a gross?
8. Feet in a pace?
9. Cubic feet in a cubic yard?
10. Pounds in a long ton?
11. Years in a millennium?
12. Cubic feet in a cord of wood?
13. Gills in a pint?

14. Degrees in a circumference?
15. Quarts in a peck?

Answers: (1) 6 (2) 2,000 (3) 4 (4)
160 (5) 231 (6) 1,760 (7) 12 (8) 3
(9) 27 (10) 2,240 (11) 1,000 (12) 128
(13) 4 (14) 360 (15) 8

■ *Statecraft:* Players rate high in "statesmanship" if they answer these correctly. Let individuals—or teams—compete.

1. Does the state of Maine or Minnesota extend farther north?
2. Which state is farthest south?
3. Which are the two smallest states?
4. Which state has the beginning of the Rio Grande?
5. Name a state that has four straight lines for boundaries.
6. Which state has Narragansett Bay?
7. Which is the only state that touches the St. Lawrence River?
8. Which state touches four of the five Great Lakes?
9. Which state borders the smallest two Great Lakes?
10. Which two states have land on both sides of the Mississippi River?
11. Which state has Kalamazoo?
12. Which state has Mobile Bay?
13. Which state has Madison for its capital?
14. Which is the Sunflower State?
15. Which state has Mount Whitney?

Answers: (1) Minnesota (2) Florida (3) Rhode Island and Delaware (4) Colorado (5) Colorado or Wyoming (6) Rhode Island (7) New York (8) Michigan (9) New York (10) Minnesota and Louisiana (11) Michigan (12) Alabama (13) Wisconsin (14) Kansas (15) California

■*Scrambled quotations:* Below is a list of common sayings, but they are disarranged into mixed up order. Ask players to straighten them out.
1. Gathers rolling no stone a moss.
2. Nine a time saves in stitch.
3. Policy best is honesty the.
4. Called few many are but chosen are.
5. Make stone not do walls prison a.
6. Fights away who lives another runs and fight to day he.
7. A will way there's where a there's.
8. Place be there's humble no like it home so ever.
9. Laughs who best laughs he last.
10. To folly where ignorance wise 'tis be bliss is.
11. Is where the home is heart.
12. Laugh alone weep and with you world and laughs the weep you.
Answers: (1) A rolling stone gathers no moss. (2) A stitch in time saves nine. (3) Honesty is the best policy. (4) Many are called but few are chosen. (5) Stone walls do not a

"*Be available to your children. Help them build a priceless ability—to see beyond the obvious, to evaluate and compare, and to create.*"

prison make. (6) He who fights and runs away lives to fight another day. (7) Where there's a will there's a way. (8) Be it ever so humble there's no place like home. (9) He who laughs last laughs best. (10) Where ignorance is bliss 'tis folly to be wise. (11) Home is where the heart is. (12) Laugh and the world laughs with you, weep and you weep alone.

■ *This language of ours:* What do the following paired-together items have in common with each other? Let players work alone or in couples.
1. A typewriter and a piano
2. Any state and a solvent business
3. A dog and a tree
4. A billiard game and an actor
5. A chimney and a bank
6. A wagon and a woman
7. An electric light and a tulip
8. An airplane and a kite
9. A bull and a trombone player
10. Our flag and a farm
11. An apple and Father's pipe
12. A fish and a grocer
13. A deck of cards and a rich man
14. Television and a door in summer
Answers: (1) Keys (2) Capital (3) Bark (4) Cue (5) Draft (6) Tongue (7) Bulb (8) Tail (9) Horn (10) Field (11) Stem (12) Scales (13) Jack (14) Screen

■ *State by state:* The problem here is to go from the state in the first column to the state in the second, traveling through only one other state. Have players name the state they would pass through.

FROM	TO
1. Tennessee	Indiana
2. Kansas	South Dakota
3. Montana	Colorado
4. Louisiana	Alabama
5. New Mexico	Idaho
6. Oklahoma	Iowa
7. Delaware	West Virginia
8. Florida	North Carolina
9. New York	Rhode Island
10. Pennsylvania	Michigan
11. Washington	California
12. Maine	Vermont
13. North Dakota	Wisconsin

Answers: (1) Kentucky (2) Nebraska (3) Wyoming (4) Mississippi (5) Utah (6) Missouri (7) Maryland (8) Georgia (9) Connecticut or Massachusetts (10) Ohio (11) Oregon (12) New Hampshire (13) Minnesota

■ *Declaration of Independence quiz:* Test players on this important document.
1. Who was the author? (a) Washington (b) Jefferson (c) Adams
2. How many signers were there? (a) 56 (b) 35 (c) 13

3. Who was the oldest signer? (a) Thomas Jefferson (b) Benjamin Franklin (c) John Adams
4. Which of the colonies had the most signers? (a) New York (b) Virginia (c) Pennsylvania
5. How many signers became a United States President? (a) three (b) two (c) one
6. Whose name became a synonym for a signature? (a) Benjamin Franklin (b) John Adams (c) John Hancock

Answers: (1) b (2) a (3) b (4) c (5) b (6) c

WORD GAMES

▪ *Make it snappy:* In the sentences below, certain words are in italics. Ask players to express these in one word, without changing the meaning of the sentence.

1. The *official enumeration of the population* takes place every ten years.
2. The letter was *seized on its way, before arrival at its destination.*
3. The last of the veterans was a *man one hundred years of age.*
4. The famous wit wrote what he wanted to be the *inscription on his tombstone.*
5. The publication was changed into a *periodical appearing every two months.*
6. The defendant furnished a *proof that he was elsewhere at the time of the crime.*

7. The barber wanted to hire a *person to take care of people's nails.*
8. The city council voted to build a *public building for the exhibition of animals living in water.*
9. All tickets for the *afternoon performance of the show* were sold out.
10. Police have a drive against *pedestrians who cross streets between intersections.*

Answers: (1) Census (2) Intercepted (3) Centenarian (4) Epitaph (5) Bi-monthly (6) Alibi (7) Manicurist (8) Aquarium (9) Matinee (10) Jaywalkers

■ *X-cues, please:* What three-letter word ending with "X" is the correct answer to each definition given?

1. Repair	7. Evening suit
2. King	8. Annoy
3. Cunning animal	9. Number
4. Loose	10. Receptacle
5. Negative answer	11. Blend
6. Bewitch	12. Levy

Answers: (1) Fix (2) Rex (3) Fox (4) Lax (5) Nix (6) Hex (7) Tux (8) Vex (9) Six (10) Box (11) Mix (12) Tax

■ *Something fishy here:* Listed below are 12 objects whose definitions spell out various kinds of fish. See how many you can guess.
1. Low singing voice
2. A celestial body

"I have too many new calendars this year. You might say I have too much time on my hands."

3. A sharp cutting tool
4. A swindler
5. A highway
6. A male ruler
7. A shiny metal
8. Sharp pointed weapon
9. Part of a shoe
10. A pet
11. Roost for birds
12. A boat canvas

Answers: (1) Bass (2) Star (3) Saw (4) Shark (5) Pike (6) King (7) Gold (8) Sword (9) Sole (10) Cat (11) Perch (12) Sail

■ *Dressing up words:* Words, like people, take a fancy to different garb. Tack the proper item of wearing onto the end of each word below, and the word will be all dressed up—as a new word. Example: Ward plus Robe is Wardrobe.

1. Rain	7. Neighbor
2. Horse	8. Ad
3. Turn	9. Lands
4. Hand	10. Law
5. Cow	11. Has
6. In	12. Fox

Answers: (1) RainBOW, RainCOAT (2) HorseSHOE (3) TurnCOAT (4) HandCUFF (5) CowSLIP (6) InVEST (7) NeighborHOOD (8) AdDRESS (9) LandsCAPE (10) LawSUIT (11) HasSOCK (12) FoxGLOVE

■*Pick the flowers:* There are a number of flowers hidden in the following poem. A flower may be in one word, or part of two or more adjoining words.

Sir, is the master still morose?
Songs of the larks pursue him close.
In the Pecos most of the skies are clear,
The crows of the cocks combine to cheer.
Yet I can name indigo, navy too,
Even lapis lazuli lacks his blue.
Let us conspire a musical spree,
With viol et cetera bring him glee.
He is now ballasting very fast
His mood to one of a pinker cast.

Answers: 1st line—iris, aster, rose 2nd— larkspur 3rd—cosmos 4th—cockscomb 5th— canna 6th—lilac 7th—spirea 8th—violet 9th—snowball 10th—pink.

■*Somebody missing:* To complete the words defined below, fill in the blank spaces with a first name or nickname. The number of blanks indicates the number of letters in the name.

1. Band– – – –   A kerchief
2. Cordu– – –   Kind of material
3. – – – –ion   A large number
4. – – – – –dore   Dock worker
5. – – –delion   Flower
6. Mac– – – –   Road building material
7. Org– – – –   Dress material
8. Big– – –   More than one spouse
9. Tis– – –   Thin paper

10. Bal– – –   Evergreen tree
11. Phan– – –   Ghost
12. – – – –et   Short coat
13. Umbr– – – –   Rain protection
14. Dis– – – – –   Bring shame upon
Answers: (1) Anna (2) Roy (3) Bill
(4) Steve (5) Dan (6) Adam (7) Andy
(8) Amy (9) Sue (10) Sam (11) Tom
(12) Jack (13) Ella (14) Grace

▪ *Letter perfect:* How many words beginning
with a certain letter can a player name in one
minute? Select any letter and ask the first
player to name as many words as he can, beginning with that letter. Time him and keep
score. Try the next player with a different letter. With the help of your dictionary you can
see which letters start the greatest number of
words. Use these most common ones.

▪ *Who knows the pros?* Guess the persons who
do the things listed below, left. Their names all
begin with PRO. The number of letters needed
is shown by dashes.

    1. Foretells   PRO– – – –
    2. Angers   PRO– – – – –
    3. Acts for another   PRO– –
    4. Sneaks around   PRO– – – –
    5. Squanders   PRO– – – – –
    6. Excels   PRO– – – –
    7. Gains unfairly   PRO– – – – – –
    8. Manufactures   PRO– – – – –

9. Hunts gold   PRO--------
10. Guards   PRO-------
11. Spreads ideas   PRO----------
12. Reminds   PRO------
13. Debases   PRO------
14. Marks corrections PRO---------
15. Objects   PRO-------

Answers: (1) Prophet (2) Provoker (3) Proxy (4) Prowler (5) Prodigal (6) Prodigy (7) Profiteer (8) Producer (9) Prospector (10) Protector (11) Propagandist (12) Prompter (13) Profaner (14) Proofreader (15) Protester

■ *Match the materials:* Match each word in the first column with one word in the second, and a fabric appears.

1. Buck	a. Cord
2. Does	b. In
3. Dam	c. Ton
4. Homes	d. Eye
5. La	e. Sucker
6. Seer	f. Ram
7. Cash	g. On
8. Sat	h. Ask
9. Whip	i. Mere
10. Birds	j. Pun
11. Ray	k. Me
12. Cot	l. Kin

Answers: (1) f (2) l (3) h (4) j (5) k (6) e (7) i (8) b (9) a (10) d (11) g (12) c

"All of us have days when we feel like a coffee bean—in a regular grind."

"*At our house, we observe Mother's Day Off. I serve the quickest meals possible (maybe two TV dinners per teen), wash dishes only once, and use the time saved to do what I want to do. Next day, I'm back on the job with new solutions to old problems.*"

Etcetera

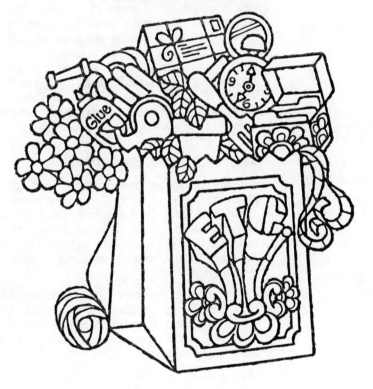

Etcetera

More ideas to use around the house, in the yard or when traveling

You never can tuck all homemaking tips into a few neat categories. There are always some odds-and-ends left over—good ideas for getting a multitude of extra chores done more easily. And that's what you'll find here. The ideas range from keeping track of appliance service calls to improvising holders when you arrange cut flowers. There's even a helpful way to keep from scratching the car if you accidentally hit the back wall of the garage. (You have to hit it gently, of course—otherwise the trick doesn't work.)

KEEPING TRACK OF THINGS

▪ Mount emergency numbers on your telephone under the receiver. Cut a piece of wide adhesive tape to fit the space on the phone and place it on a piece of waxed paper. Use a ball-point pen to print names and numbers on the tape. Remove waxed paper and press the tape in place.

▪ Keep a house directory handy and in plain sight for friends, neighbors or baby-sitters to use in an emergency. List locations of such items as first-aid supplies, fuses, flashlight and fire extinguishers.

▪ Clip a couple of plain sheets of paper to the inside back cover of your telephone directory. Notepaper will always be ready for jotting down a message.

- Put alphabetical envelope-style dividers in a loose-leaf notebook to file guarantees, instruction books and care tags for your appliances and furnishings.

- Glue a miniature calendar to the inside cover of your checkbook for handy reference.

- A perk-up inventory is good for the home and the homemaker. Go through the house and make two lists. On one sheet of paper, write down things to do (touch up a table leg, wash the lampshades); on another, note things to buy (shelf lining, shower curtain). Hang the first list in your kitchen for spare-time reference. Put the second in your purse as a shopping reminder.

- Compile a master list for grocery shopping, including brand names and sizes. Use it to make a fast check of the pantry and cabinets for your weekly shopping trips.

- If you have someone away from home, attending school or working, copy this idea from a North Dakota family. They keep a large calendar in the kitchen and record interesting things that happen each day. At the end of the month, they tear off the page and send it to the one who is away.

Or tack a large manila envelope to the kitchen bulletin board. You can drop in messages to be mailed periodically as a collection of small letters.

"Many household aids come in cans of similar sizes, shapes and colors. Some say, 'Shake before using'; others say, 'Don't shake.' To avoid reading directions each time, print a large S on cans that do need shaking."

■ Copy addresses of family and friends on 3×5″ index cards filed alphabetically. It's easy to add names or change addresses, and there's room for birth dates, anniversaries, food likes and dislikes.

■ Use a tiny three-ring binder as an address book. You can carry a small one in your purse, and the pages can be replaced easily to keep up with any changes.

■ Keep a card file on appliance repairs. Besides the model number, record the serviceman's telephone number, the date of his last visit, the repairs he made and the charge.

Or attach a stick-on label to each major appliance. Use a label large enough so you can record date of last service call and the repairman's telephone number. Labels are easy to update or replace.

■ If you have a large family calendar, write down dates for each person in a different color —red for Mom, blue for Dad, etc.

■ When your telephone directory includes numbers for several communities, mark the book so you can find your exchange quickly. Open the directory to the page where your exchange starts. Cut off the upper corners of all the preceding pages.

■ A tin-can secretary is the handiest gadget in her kitchen, claims a California woman. It's a

No. 2 can with lid removed, and it holds a pen, pencils, laundry marker, scissors and a tube of glue. A small stapler and a few paper clips hang on the rim; rubber bands circle the can. The homemaker covered the can with self-adhesive plastic.

■ Make a master list of the contents of your safety deposit box at the bank, and keep it at home for reference. Saves time when you need to locate an important paper.

■ Do you know what credit cards and identification papers you carry in your wallet? Make a list with information about each item. Include the identification number, expiration date and the address you should write in case the card or paper is lost.

■ Fasten clippings in a scrapbook with pieces of clear plastic (cut from a plastic bag). Put plastic between page and clipping; press with iron set for wool. Clippings will not discolor, pages won't warp.

■ When you mount a snapshot in your photograph album, put the negative behind the print. You'll know exactly where it is. (Be careful not to scratch or damage the negative.)

■ Make it easy to locate shut-off valves in your home. Mark all hot water pipes with one color, cold water pipes with another and gas lines with a third color.

■ Make a diagram of your fuse box, and note which fixtures and appliances are on each fuse. Keep the information near the box.

PACKING AND MAILING

■ Plastic bags filled with excelsior or shredded paper make good "pillows" to cushion breakable items that you wrap for mailing. Or save plastic dry cleaning bags to use as space fillers in mailing cartons.

Another idea is to line the inside of a firm packing box with empty egg cartons, then surround the object generously with crumpled paper so it won't shift inside the box. You have a shockproof wrap.

■ When mailing a package to a foreign country, cover it with two or three wrappings, each one tied and addressed separately. Should the outside wrapper be torn off in shipping, the addresses on the inner wrappers will get the package to its destination.

■ As you wrap packages for mailing, you can cut V-notches on the box edges where the cord goes. This prevents cord from slipping.

■ Protect a fancy gift bow for mailing by covering the bow with the lid of another box. Then wrap the package in heavy paper.

■ Tuck in a long piece of dental floss when you send a cake to a child at camp. The dental floss can be used to cut the cake; there is no need for a knife.

■ Next time you write for information and must enclose a self-addressed envelope, do this. Write your request on the enclosed envelope—inside the flap. Then fold the flap back so it points to your name and address.

■ Use postcards to encourage correspondence. Give a pack of self-addressed postcards to your youngster who goes off to camp or college; he has only to add the messages. Keep another pack handy so you can write to elderly friends and relatives. They'll enjoy regular postcards more than infrequent letters.

■ Jot down most-used addresses on the inside of your stationery box cover. Also, glue an envelope for holding stamps and labels to the inside of that cover.

■ To make sure you don't forget birthdays, address your cards on the first of each month and write the mailing date in the corner where the stamp belongs. When it's time to mail the letter, add the stamp and send it.

■ You can separate stamps and envelopes that get stuck together in humid weather. Place a slightly damp piece of paper on top of the stamps, and run a hot iron quickly over the paper. Separate the stamps or envelope flaps before the glue cools.

"I have known women who were overly concerned about housework, and when they did get away from home, what did they talk about? You guessed it. Housework!"

- Protect an address label from moisture by painting over it with colorless nail polish. This is especially good for packages going a long distance.

- To send coins by mail, slit small pockets between the layers of medium-thick cardboard that is cut to the size of the envelope. Slip a coin into each pocket.

WHEN YOU DRIVE

- A shower curtain ring that closes like a safety pin makes a good inexpensive key holder. Put a couple of safety pins on the ring so you're always ready for an emergency.

- Keep an old window shade (rolled up) in your car trunk for emergencies. If trouble occurs and you must kneel on the ground, use the shade to protect clothing.

- A large discarded purse makes a splendid automobile first-aid and sewing kit. If it is left in the car, you are always ready to dress a small cut or sew up a ripped seam.

- Keep a small magnet under the ignition switch on the car to hold errand reminders or turnpike toll tickets.

- Sew a small magnet to each cuff of your driving gloves. Touch magnets to the dashboard of the car after each trip; they'll cling there until you need them again.

■ Carry a small magnifying glass in the glove compartment of the car—for map reading.

■ A large manila envelope can be slipped over the car visor and used as an extension to keep the sun out of your eyes.

■ If you carry a blanket in the car, make a cotton zippered slipcover to keep it clean. Then the blanket can double as a pillow.

■ For winter driving, put a gallon plastic jug filled with dry sand in your car trunk. It's easy to handle when you're on an icy spot.

■ Make bumper guards for the back wall of your garage. Cut an old rubber tire across the middle. Fasten the two halves, with cut ends in, across the wall at the same height as the car bumpers. Protects car from scratches.

■ Carry a small travel alarm clock in your purse when you shop, as an Illinois woman does. She sets it to ring just before the parking meter expires.

■ Keep last year's phone book in the car. You can check addresses when you run errands.

■ When you're through with a plastic bottle of dishwashing detergent, fill it with water and put it in the car. You have soapy water for emergency hand washing.

■ A spring-type clothespin holds eyeglasses to the sun visor when you're not wearing them.

TRIPPING AND CAMPING

▪ Pack an empty fold-up tote bag for your trip. It doesn't take much room and it's handy for carrying things you accumulate.

▪ Take along several process-by-mail envelopes for film. As you expose a roll, mail it for processing. By the time you get home, some of your pictures may be waiting for you.

▪ Large brown mailing envelopes can be useful on a trip. Use them to send home literature and pamphlets you collect. Good idea if you have to carry your own luggage.

▪ To save time on a long trip, type addresses of friends and family on perforated gummed labels. Tear off labels to paste on postcards and packages along the way. Labels help you keep track of cards yet to be sent.

▪ You can use worn-out socks to pull over and protect shoes you pack for travel.

▪ Carry a few spring-type clothespins while traveling to hang up skirts and trousers.

▪ For a short motor trip, you can use a plastic raincoat as a garment bag. Just button the coat over dresses and suits and hang everything in the car.

▪ Keep neckties unwrinkled by packing them between the pages of a magazine.

■ Before starting an extended camping trip, try an overnight stay in a nearby campground or in the backyard. This "rehearsal" alerts you to items you might have left at home.

■ If your cooking oil is in a glass bottle, transfer it to an unbreakable container for a camping trip.

■ If you vacation in a tent, a Michigan homemaker suggests taking along an accessory bag fitted with shelves designed to hold shoes or handbags. It keeps lightweight dishes, silverware, cereal and other foods clean and safe from insects. Shelves can be covered with self-adhesive plastic for easy cleaning.

■ When camping out, fasten strips of blotting paper soaked in insect repellent around cot and table legs to keep ants and other crawling insects out of beds and off tables.

■ Use leftover paint to color-key tent poles. Saves time when you set up camp.

■ Line the bottom of an outdoor grill with a layer of heavy-duty foil (or two layers of regular foil). Lining reflects heat from coals, makes removal of ashes easy and leaves the grill clean.

■ Keep a combination can-and-bottle opener in the glove compartment of your car. You'll always have it with you—for a quick picnic or a long vacation tour.

"Frustrated housewives are missing a point. We marry husbands, not houses."

■ Cut down the legs of an old card table and take it along for sit-on-the-ground picnics. It's fine for serving meals at the beach—keeps sand out of the food.

GARDENING—INDOORS AND OUT

■ To rinse the leaves of house plants under a faucet without washing away the soil, make a plastic bib for the pot. Cut the plastic several inches larger than the top of the pot, and make a slit to the center. Then cut a hole in the center of the bib, large enough to fit around the plant stems. Slip the bib over the top of the pot; fasten it in place with a spring-type clothespin.

■ Make a dainty cultivator for breaking up soil close to African violets or small, new garden plants. Spread tines of an old dinner fork and bend them upward in the middle.

■ Small seeds for indoor planting are easy to handle if you pick them up with a wet matchstick. Seeds cling to the end of the stick and can be planted exactly where you want them. Twirl match against soil to release seeds.

■ Start plants, without transplanting, in a miniature greenhouse. Plant a cutting or leaf in a porous pot filled with the soil you would use for the growing plant. Water, and cover with a plastic bag punched with a few holes. Hold bag in place with a rubber band around the rim of the pot. Be sure bag doesn't crowd leaves. Set pot where light is adequate but not in direct sunlight. Moisture collects on inside of bag. This method keeps stems firm, and leaves won't turn black. Check soil every few days; water when dry.

▪ Dig up some of your best topsoil before the ground freezes. You can use it for repotting plants during the winter. Store soil in plastic bags or other dry containers.

▪ A meat baster, with its glass or plastic tube and rubber syringe top, makes a handy gadget for watering plants, especially those in the base of a lamp or hanging on the wall. Use it also for changing water in a vase without disturbing the flower arrangement.

▪ Keep a garden scrapbook with a map of your yard on which you locate all plantings. Include labels and instructions for seeds and plants you buy; clip pictures and descriptions from seed catalogs to illustrate plantings that friends give you. The scrapbook is a ready reference when you need to know how to care for a plant or how old it is.

▪ During the blooming period of your flower garden, take color photographs of the perennials, such as iris, phlox and chrysanthemums. When ready to divide and transplant, you know what colors you are moving.

R

■ Use a child's toy rake for hard-to-reach places in your garden. It's lightweight, and you can handle it when you're on your knees.

■ Work garden tools up and down in oily sand to clean and protect them from rust when you're through for the day. Store mixture of sand and oil in a covered container.

■ Built-in knee pads add comfort when you weed the garden. Sew large pockets on knees of old slacks and insert pieces of foam.

■ Use a salt shaker for planting small seeds, either vegetable or flower. Better distribution this way, and work goes fast.

■ When setting out tiny plants in flats or beds, use an apple corer to take them up for transplanting. No trowel is small enough, and a knife doesn't do the job as well.

■ As you transplant tomatoes, put a tin can (with top and bottom cut out) over each plant. Step on can to leave an inch out of the ground. The can shields the plant from wind and keeps cutworms from the stems. When plant is a few weeks old, remove the can.

■ Water newly transplanted trees and shrubs by placing at the base of the plant a large container that has several small holes in the bottom. Fill the container with water as often as necessary to keep the surrounding area damp. A discarded, leaky bucket is fine.

▪ To train ivy as a ground cover, fasten the runners against the ground with wire hairpins until the ivy takes root.

▪ If flower stems are too short when making flower arrangements, insert them in plastic drinking straws; trim to proper length for your vase. Be sure flower stems reach water.

▪ If you don't have a regular flower frog for doing arrangements, you can improvise. A scouring pad of loose plastic loops will fit into a small container to hold flowers.

Or put sand in a bowl or vase and push flower stems down into it; keep sand moist. This helps prevent vase from tipping, too.

▪ To arrange long-stemmed flowers, put transparent tape crisscross over a wide-mouth vase.

▪ Broken flower stems mended with transparent tape will last as long as unbroken ones.

▪ Keep cut flowers fresh when using a few in a table arrangement of other materials. Put a little water in a small toy balloon and insert several sprigs of flowers; fasten balloon securely with a rubber band. Hide the balloon in the arrangement so that only the blossoms show.

ENTERTAINING TIPS

▪ Plan to entertain different guests several days in a row. Then silver, best glassware and

"I was delivering another basket of cucumbers to a neighbor when her young son looked at my basket and said, 'Oh goody, little ones.' I asked if he liked small ones better, and he answered, 'Yes, Mommy can't get the big ones down the garbage disposer.'"

dishes need to be taken out, polished and stored away only once. You can use the same flowers and centerpieces—and the same menu —for all the events.

■ Expand your small dining table for company dinners by covering it with a 4×8′ section of plywood. After centering the plywood on the table, mark the table outline on it. Cut off small triangles from corners; mount the pieces (with nails or glue) along the table markings on the bottom side to keep the plywood from sliding.

■ You can set a tray table beside the hostess' chair to hold rolls and relishes that are passed during the meal. Use the tray also in serving dessert or coffee.

■ Use a 30-cup coffee maker for serving cold drinks to a large crowd. With the coffee basket removed, there's plenty of room for ice. Turning the spigot is easier than dipping from a punch bowl.

■ Use a colored sheet under your lace table-cloth to change the appearance of your table.

■ Next time you have a party, make a center-piece of the prizes to be given. You might place a bare tree branch in a container, then tie small colorfully wrapped prizes to the tree. When a guest wins a game, have him choose a surprise prize.

■ When entertaining a crowd, you can use a punch bowl to hold the tossed salad.

■ When you entertain dinner guests, use your automatic oven timer to remind you to look at potatoes, check the roast or put on vegetables. It saves extra trips to the kitchen and eliminates clock watching.

■ To help first-time guests find your house at night, replace the porch or outside light bulb with a green or yellow one. Tell your guests to look for the colored light.

GIFT IDEAS

■ Keep a few house plants for an inexpensive gift at a wedding shower or birthday party. A pretty pot and ribbon add a special touch.

■ A camera helps you give a special gift to a bride. When you're invited to a wedding shower, take your camera and flashbulbs along. Snap candid pictures of the bride-to-be, the gifts and the serving table. Make a book of these pictures for the bride.

■ Practical gifts for children bring more pleasure if there's a surprise tucked inside. For instance, each finger of a pair of gloves might hold a small coin.

■ Homemade gift coupons are an inexpensive but thoughtful gift for children to give to their parents or grandparents. Coupons might read: "Good for one car wash, lawn mowing or other chore." Make them with colored paper, felt pens and crayons.

■ For baby showers, decorate a diaper pail and fill it with small items (such as baby powder, lotion and pins) a new mother needs.

■ Mark family birthdays on a gift calendar— place gold stars on the days to remember. Makes a good present for a grandparent.

■ To give a magazine subscription as a gift, cut out name of magazine, along with interesting titles or paragraphs from a past issue. Glue these on paper. On the other side, write a greeting and note about your gift. Roll with titles out, and tie.

■ For a shut-in, decorate a Christmas gift tray. Anchor a centerpiece—maybe a tree-shaped evergreen branch with florist's clay, then decorate the branch. Wrap small presents and place around "tree."

■ Make a money tree for a Golden Wedding Anniversary. Plant several small branches in a flower pot. Paint pot and tree gold and cover soil with moss or flowers. Hang on tree coins or bills rolled in gold paper and tied with gold ribbon. For a Silver Anniversary, use a silvered tree and silver dollars (or foil-wrapped coins).

"Amy won't tell us what she wants for Christmas. She says she'll tell Santa at the department store, and we'll find out Christmas morning."